LIGHT OF
THE WORLD

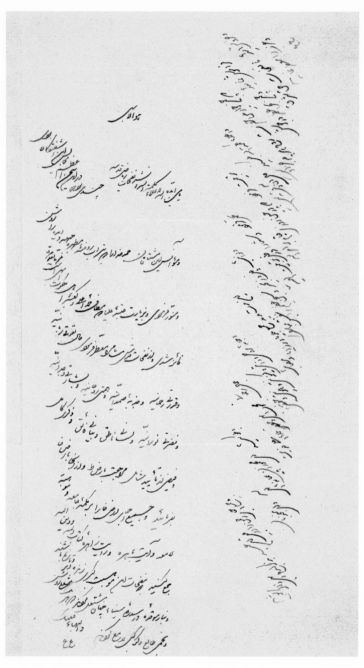

A Tablet of 'Abdu'l-Bahá in His own handwriting, the translation of which appears as no. 49 in this volume. © Bahá'í World Centre.

LIGHT OF THE WORLD

Selected Tablets of 'Abdu'l-Bahá

BAHÁ'Í WORLD CENTRE

HAIFA

Preface

On 29 May 1892, after four decades of bountiful radiance, from the first intimation of its rising glory in the Síyáh-Chál and Baghdad to its midday splendour in Adrianople and 'Akká, the Sun of Bahá—as 'Abdu'l-Bahá memorably relayed in His telegram informing Sultán 'Abdu'l-Ḥamíd of the ascension of Bahá'u'lláh—had set. Yet the setting of that Sun was not followed by the dark of night but by the reflection of its glory in the Moon of the Covenant, lighting the path ahead, towards the attainment of Bahá'u'lláh's ultimate purpose: the unification of humanity.

As the radiant Centre of that Covenant, 'Abdu'l-Bahá, Bahá'u'lláh's eldest son and appointed Successor, would, for the next three decades, lead the Cause and be "the steward of its glory and the diffuser of its light". His mission would be "to enrich and extend the bounds of the incorruptible patrimony entrusted to His hands by shedding the illumination of His Father's Faith upon the West, by expounding the fundamental precepts of that Faith and its cardinal principles, by consolidating the activities which had already been initiated for the promotion of its interests, and, finally, by ushering in, through the provisions of His own Will, the Formative Age in its evolution".[1]

Over the course of that unique stewardship, 'Abdu'l-Bahá wrote thousands of Tablets to individuals and communities in the East and the West, comprising an unceasing outpouring of guidance, encouragement, sustenance, edification, and boundless love. The present volume consists of seventy-six newly translated selections chosen from Tablets originally published in Persian in volumes 3 and 4 of *Muntakhabátí az Makátíb-i-Ḥaḍrat-i-'Abdu'l-Bahá*. Though the Tablets presented here cover the entire period of 'Abdu'l-Bahá's ministry, many were written soon after the "Supreme Affliction" of the passing of Bahá'u'lláh. At that moment, the orphaned community of the Greatest Name, grief-stricken and despondent, turned to 'Abdu'l-Bahá, recognizing Him to be, "in its hour of desperate need, its Solace, its Guide, its Mainstay and Champion".[2]

Whether writing to the friends at that time of bereavement, or in later years when they found themselves suffering persecution and hardship, 'Abdu'l-Bahá called them to reflect on the life of the Blessed Beauty, Whose "one and only purpose in accepting such trials and tribulations for His blessed Self was to instruct the lovers in the ways of love and teach the longing souls the art of servitude". The loved ones of God, 'Abdu'l-Bahá wrote, must "not be grieved or distressed at these countless afflictions, for in bearing such trials, they share in the sufferings of the Abhá Beauty".

The Tablets in this volume provide a selection, in English translation, chosen from among many written by

'Abdu'l-Bahá that recount aspects of the life of Bahá'u'lláh and the tribulations He endured, events in His homeland, the purpose and greatness of His Cause, the unparalleled nature and significance of His Covenant—as well as the attempts of its enemies to subvert and destroy it—and some of the Biblical and Quranic allusions and prophecies about the Blessed Beauty. Reflected in many of the Tablets are parallels between Bahá'u'lláh's sufferings at the hands of His adversaries and the afflictions 'Abdu'l-Bahá was similarly made to endure.

These Tablets are thus doubly precious: Who better to tell us about Bahá'u'lláh, and to impart to us His "lessons of the spirit in the school of insight", than His most cherished Son, Who shared, as His closest associate, His life of exile, imprisonment, and persecution, and Who, titled by His Father the "Mystery of God", stood in a unique relationship to the Author of the Revelation as "the image of His perfections", "the Interpreter of His mind", "the Focal Point of His unerring guidance", "the stainless mirror reflecting His light"?[3]

The lapse of a century since the passing of 'Abdu'l-Bahá only testifies to His words of assurance that the Sun of Bahá'u'lláh's Revelation "shall never set, nor shall that Day-Star of the Realm of Glory ever wane.... It remaineth ever shining in its meridian splendour, ever glowing and luminous, at the sublime apex of bounty."

LIGHT OF
THE WORLD

I

He is the All-Glorious.

O friends! How blessed, how favoured, how fortunate ¹ are ye to have been born in such a cycle and dispensation and to live in such an age and century, to have come upon such a wellspring and bowed down before such a threshold, to have taken shelter beneath the shade of such a tree and partaken of such a fruit. The cycle is the Cycle of the Ancient Beauty, and the century that of the Greatest Name. The wellspring is the stream of the Law of God, and the threshold that of the Abhá Beauty. The tree is the Tree of Life, and the fruit that of the Divine Lote-Tree. Blessed are they that attain thereunto! Fortunate are they that enter therein! Gladdened are they that draw nigh unto it! And happy are they that abide under its shade! All praise be to God, the Lord of the worlds. Convey my warmest Abhá greetings to all the friends....

2

He is God.

O thou seeker after truth! Behold the power and great- ¹ ness of Bahá'u'lláh! Within a short span of time, He hath stirred up the East and the West, and raised aloft, in the midmost heart of the world, the banner of love and harmony, of unity and peace, of fellowship and conciliation, of truthfulness and rectitude. He hath freed from enmity and strife a great multitude of souls belonging to divers and opposing nations, to disparate and contending religions, and hath brought them under the sheltering canopy of fellowship, love, and unity.

2 What power this is, and what strength! What greater proof couldst thou desire? He hath brought East and West into close embrace. Singly and alone, He hath withstood the world and uplifted His mighty Cause in the Most Great Prison. Though subjected to utter abasement, He hath crowned His loved ones with the diadem of everlasting glory. Were one to gaze with the eye of justice, this would be sufficient proof.

3 Thou hast written concerning the cost of postage. 'Abdu'l-Bahá hath offered up his life for thee, how much more his earthly possessions! Upon thee be greetings and praise.

3

God is the All-Glorious.

1 O ye true friends and loved ones of God! The Candle shineth resplendent, and the century of the Abhá Beauty is even as a flowering rose-garden. The dawn

of the Abhá Kingdom hath broken, and the stars of the celestial Concourse glow with light. Gentle breezes blow from the meads of the Lord, and sweet savours waft from the gardens of holiness. Heavenly strains from the Kingdom of glory are raised on every side, and the summons of the Company on high reacheth the ears of every lowly one. The Day-Star of divine bounty hath risen in all its splendour, and the Orb of God's grace sheddeth its radiance upon all regions. The manifold bounties of the Most Great Name—may my life be offered up for His loved ones—are all-embracing, and the banquet table of the Lord is spread throughout the earth. These blessings indeed compass you on every side.

Behold, then, what a diadem of bounty adorneth 2 your heads and what a kingly mantle attireth your beings. Consider what eyes of bounty watch over you and what glances of mercy are cast upon you. Wherefore, be not saddened by the cruelty of the peoples of the world or grieved by relentless trials. For all these befall you in the path of the Ancient Beauty; all these ye suffer for the sake of the Most Great Name. These tribulations are bountiful gifts, and these afflictions naught but manifold bestowals. This captivity is kingship, and this prison a lofty palace. This blame and condemnation is praise and commendation, and this chain a necklace of world-embracing sovereignty. These stocks and fetters are the adornment of the feet of every fortunate one, these bonds and shackles are the highest hope of the people of glory, and these blades and swords the ultimate desire of the lovers of the resplendent Beauty.

3   Consider how the sacred breast of the Exalted One— may my life be a sacrifice unto Him—was made a target for a hundred thousand bullets, and how the holy body of Quddús—may my life be offered up for Him—was torn to pieces. Consider the galling of the chains and fetters that weighed upon the blessed neck of the Most Great Name—may my soul be offered up for His loved ones— and how He was taken, in that condition, bare-headed and bare-footed, all the way from Níyávarán to Ṭihrán. Many a trial befell that Sacred Beauty for well-nigh fifty years, such that the pen trembleth at their mention. The first was the exile from Persia; the second, the banishment from Iraq to the Ottoman capital; the third, the exile from that city to European Turkey and Bulgaria;[4] and the fourth, the banishment of the Beauty of the All-Merciful to the depths of the Most Great Prison. Throughout this period, a myriad other tribulations also befell Him from within and without.

4   Likewise, call thou to mind the Bábu'l-Báb[5]—may the souls of the well-favoured of the Lord be offered up for him—and consider what trials and tribulations that luminous candle and radiant orb suffered, and what woes he endured in the path of God. Consider how, in the fort of adversity, he finally quaffed the brimful cup of martyrdom, and what injuries were inflicted upon his kin.

5   Recall, too, those other blessed souls who were even as

shining lamps unto this world, as brilliant stars among the children of men, as resplendent rays and luminous orbs. They sacrificed themselves, one and all, and shone brightly in the path of the Blessed Beauty. They suffered captivity and endured fierce persecution, were pillaged and plundered, were cast into prisons and dungeons, until, in utter meekness, they drank at last the draught of martyrdom.

It is therefore clear and evident that the trials endured ⁶ in the path of the Friend are the ardent desire of such as are nigh unto Him, that woes suffered for the sake of the Lord are the sole yearning of the denizens of the realms above. Though to outward seeming they are poison, in reality they are pure honey. And though bitter on the lips of those who waver, they are sweet as sugar to those who stand firm. Therefore, in gratitude for such a bounty, in appreciation for the afflictions and trials ye have endured in the path of the incomparable Beloved, it behoveth you to arise with such zeal and fervour as to dazzle the minds of all who dwell on earth. The glory of God rest upon each and every one of you, O ye beloved of the Lord.

4

He is the All-Glorious.

1 O ye beloved of the Merciful! The Abhá Beauty hath shone forth with His manifold names and attributes from the Dawning-Point of all desires. He hath caused this glorious century to become the revealer of His wondrous grace through the effulgence of this new light, and hath set aglow the candle of unity in the world of being. In sweet accents of oneness and in celestial melodies proclaiming Divine Unity, He hath warbled upon the branches of the garden of inner meanings so as to gather the scattered peoples of the world under the shadow of the Word of God and bring the hostile and contentious tribes of the earth together in unity and harmony beneath the canopy of the love of God. For this exalted aim, this sanctified and manifest purpose, He hath offered His breast to a myriad darts of woe, and welcomed countless wounds with utter joy and resignation, even as a healing balm.

2 Not for an instant did He rest; not for a moment did His sacred heart find tranquillity. How many a night did He pass under the weight of chains, enduring until dawn a hundred thousand hardships, even as a captive seized within a hostile land. He met the darts of injustice with the target of faithfulness, and quaffed the poison of affliction as if it were the honeyed draught of immortality. He kissed the sharpened blade as though it were a brimming

cup, and fervently yearned for the harrowing prison as if it were a loving embrace. He was exiled from His land and became a wanderer in the wilderness of adversity. He was banished to Iraq and Adrianople, and was finally incarcerated in the most desolate of cities. At last, despite all these afflictive calamities and toilsome tribulations, He planted the Tree of Oneness in the paradise of this new Cycle and raised the tabernacle of unity, peace, and reconciliation above the highest of all standards.

Then did the morn of hope dawn and the Sun of 3 Truth begin to shine. Its light was shed upon all regions, and the morning breeze wafted forth. The joyful tidings of the Revelation were announced, and the blazing flame and glowing fire of the Burning Bush shone resplendent. The billows of the ocean of unity, even as the hosts of guidance, beat upon the shores of discord and cast the precious pearls of unity and concord far and wide. The divine springtime encircled the earth, heavenly flowers bloomed, vernal showers rained down, and life-bestowing winds blew on every side, till at last all were filled with hope that the beauty of Oneness would be unveiled in the assemblage of the world, and that the brightness of its countenance would shine resplendent throughout all regions.

Wherefore, O ye beloved of the Lord and friends of 4 God, arise, and with the whole enthusiasm of your hearts, with all the eagerness of your souls, strive to unfurl the standards of unity in the midmost heart of the world and cause, with valiant might, the ocean of oneness to surge. Thus may the body of humankind be freed from the constraint of these variegated robes and patched garments, and be adorned instead with the sanctified raiment of unity.

5   This is the principal aim and true purpose of the revelation of the Prophets, the advent of the chosen Ones, and the rising of the Sun of Reality in this most great Dispensation of the King of Glory. Unless this sublime aim be achieved, unless this purpose of the All-Glorious Lord be fulfilled and made manifest in the assemblage of the world, this great Cycle will prove idle and this mighty Dispensation will yield no fruit. God grant that all endeavours may be dedicated to establishing the ties of unity and concord.

6   The glory of God rest upon all who are steadfast in the Covenant and have clung to that holy Testament, through which God shieldeth against all discord.

5

1   O servant of the one true God! When the Morn of divine guidance dawned above the Most Exalted Horizon, its rays brought tidings of great joy and heralded the advent of the Abhá Beauty, as is openly and unequivocally stated in the Qayyúmu'l-Asmá'.

2   In the whole of the Bayán, all things find their consummation in these wondrous and sublime words: "The

Day of Resurrection is from the time of the dawning of the Sun of Bahá until its setting."[6] "Beware, beware, lest the Váḥid of the Bayán shut thee out as by a veil from Him. And beware, beware, that what hath been sent down in the Bayán shut thee not out as by a veil from Him."[7] The Báb Himself is among the Váḥid of the Bayán: There are the eighteen Letters of the Living, and He Himself is the nineteenth. One of the Letters of the Living is Quddús, of whom He hath said that Mirrors to the number of thirteen Váḥids abide beneath his shadow.[8]

Therefore, say unto them that are veiled: "The Exalted 3 One hath warned you to beware, beware, lest by turning unto Him or unto that which hath been revealed in the Bayán ye be shut out as by a veil from the Beauty of the Lord. Yet ye foolish ones are raising a clamour on every side. One saith, 'Where is the advent of Him Whom God shall make manifest?' while another exclaimeth, 'Where are His palaces?' One asketh, 'Where is the primary school of Him Whom God shall make manifest?'[9] and yet another demandeth, 'Where is the cradle of His resurrection?'"

The Báb Himself saith: "Beware lest the Váḥid of the 4 Bayán and that which hath been revealed in the Bayán shut thee out as by a veil from Him." And yet, notwithstanding this, these foolish ones have seized upon the outer meaning of the verses as a pretext to cavil against that peerless Beauty in Whose praise the whole of the Bayán hath been revealed. "What aileth these people that they come not close to understanding what is said unto them?"[10] He hath also said: "Were He to appear at this very moment, I would be the first to adore Him." And again: "In the year nine ye shall attain unto all good." And so on.

5   First, consider the basis on which they pronounced the death sentence against the Most Exalted One, the Báb—may my life be a sacrifice unto Him! Mullá Muḥammad-i-Mamaqání cried out, "O people! In the Qur'án God saith: 'No doubt is there about this Book: It is a guidance unto the God-fearing';[11] that is, it guideth aright all humanity. It is also clearly stated: 'But He is the Apostle of God and the Seal of the Prophets.'[12] How can we regard such an explicit statement as the source of error, while it is guidance itself? This person who claimeth to be a descendant of the Prophet hath indeed destroyed the foundation laid down by Him!" He then mentioned, one by one, some of the laws revealed in the Bayán—laws that were later abrogated in the Kitáb-i-Aqdas. Thereupon, he ordered the emblem of the Báb's noble lineage to be removed from His head,[13] and issued, without hesitation and with the utmost malice, the sentence of His death.

6   Say: Unto what did the Jewish people cleave except the outer meanings of the verses of the Torah when they adorned the cross with the body of the Beloved, thus depriving themselves of the grace of the Messiah? They clung unto the literal text of the Torah while remaining veiled from Him Who was its Revealer. The Pharisees, who ranked among the most learned of that age and cycle, called Christ not Messiah [Masíḥ] but a monster [Masíkh].

They regarded His comely and beauteous Countenance as vile and unsightly. Such are the ways of the people at the hour of the dawning of the Day-Star of the world.

Likewise, when the breezes of the Revelation of 7 Muḥammad perfumed the regions of Mecca and Medina, and the reviving breaths of the divine Teachings made the Arabian Peninsula the scene of the celestial springtide, the Christian divines also clung unto the literal interpretation of God's perspicuous Book and remained deprived of the splendours of the Day-Star of the realms above. For according to the outward meaning of the text of the Holy Gospel, there will be no other advent after Christ. The priests and clerics held fast unto these words and remained veiled from the light of certitude that shone forth from the luminous Horizon.

In brief, on the day of the Revelation of the divine 8 Light, the peoples of the world invariably cleaved unto the outward meanings of the verses of the Book, and thus deprived themselves of the grace of the Almighty. Worse still, most of the divines used their interpretation of the Holy Books to decree the death of these sovereign Lords of all existence, these Luminaries of the visible and invisible realms. Yet, there is little cause for wonder that those peoples were veiled from the Lord of creation, for their Holy Books and Scriptures did not contain such clear and explicit counsels and such conclusive admonitions as are found in the Bayán.

But the Báb—may my life be offered up for Him— 9

left no soul any room for hesitation. He removed the veils completely. Throughout the Bayán, He openly and unambiguously declared that the object of all the Scriptures and sacred Books was none other than the Most Great Light. He warned the people to beware lest they be veiled from the Day-Star of the world by the text of the Book, or by their own interpretations of the verses and utterances. Were counsels and admonitions such as these ever revealed in the Torah, the Gospel, or the Holy Qur'án? Nay, by the righteousness of God! This is unique to this Most Great Dispensation, in which the Morn of divine guidance, the Most Exalted Beauty—may my life be offered up for Him—hath rent asunder the concealing veils and made the path of guidance plain and clear.

10 Moreover, following the martyrdom of that Mystery of existence, that glorious Being, where were these perverse people to be found? Each had crept into the corner of everlasting abasement, turned away from friend and stranger alike, and, seized with fear and trepidation, remained hidden from everyone until such time as the Ancient Beauty, the Most Great Name—may my life be offered up for His loved ones—exalted the Cause of God. Then it was that these creeping things crawled out of their hiding places and flaunted themselves. In no time at all, they stirred up mischief, raised the banner of hatred, and thus cast themselves into the abyss of woeful torment. No mention dost thou hear from them now, nor the faintest murmur.[14]

11 Consider more recent events. When these exiles were

under the threat of the sword, the King of Martyrs and the Beloved of Martyrs—may my life be offered up for them both—as well as other martyrs, attained the station of supreme sacrifice. The martyrs in Yazd were ripped to pieces, and those in <u>Kh</u>urásán were burnt to death, their dust and ashes scattered to the winds. So too it was in <u>Sh</u>íráz and other parts of the country. At that same time, the leader of these wayward people expressly repudiated the Báb from the pulpits of Iṣfahán and Ṭihrán.[15] Can this also be denied, though it had become the talk of both towns?

Now that he is witnessing how the praises of the Cause [12] of God have set the East and the West in motion, how the fame of the Most Great Name hath encompassed the North and the South, how the potency of the Word of God hath shaken the powers of the world, and how the divine Call, bearing the joyful tidings of the Spirit, hath quickened and revitalized the world of humanity—he hath once again emerged from his pit of obscurity. He hath raised an uproar and asserted his existence, declaring: "We are the people of the Bayán, and the cornerstone of this edifice."

Far, far be it from the truth! Where were these people [13] a few years ago? Who amongst them hath ever quaffed from the cup of tribulation or exerted the least effort in the pathway of the Exalted One? Naught have they ever manifested but denial and repudiation; nothing have they ever shown save indecency and vice. By God, besides

Whom there is none other! Should there now be any test or trial, ye would immediately witness them ascending the pulpit and raising the cry of "We are wholly quit of them!"[16] Nay, they would curse and revile the Cause of God....

14 Consider how the burning meteor of the Covenant hath pierced the heart of the world. Witness the rays that stream forth from the unseen Kingdom upon the lands of the Slavs and the Turks.

> Shed splendours on the Orient,
> And perfumes scatter in the West,
> Carry light unto the Slav,
> And the Turk with life invest.

And yet these deniers, even as the bats of darkness, have crawled into their caves of apathy and deny the existence of the sun. How well hath it been said:

> Granted that this morn be called a darksome night,
> Are seeing eyes also blinded by the light?[17]

15 Nay, by the righteousness of the Lord! Erelong thou shalt hear the sound of this Bugle and the blasts of this Trumpet coming from the Concourse on high. Glory be to my Lord, the All-Glorious! Upon thee be greetings and praise.

LIGHT OF THE WORLD

6

He is God.

O Lord, my God, my Best-Beloved, my Aim, my heart's ¹
Desire! This, verily, is the first of the days of Riḍván.
It is come with joy and delight, exultation and rapture.
The winds are wafting, the clouds are raining down, and
the sun is shining forth through Thy bountiful grace. The
morning breeze bloweth over hill and dale in this wondrous Springtime, as a token of Thine inestimable favour,
transforming these lands into a fine brocade of incomparable hues and a silken carpet begemmed with flowers
and adorned with a vesture of verdant leaves that dazzle
the eyes with their gleaming splendour. The breezes blow
gently, the fresh streams flow softly, and the meads are
adorned with bloom; the groves are lush, the clouds
are rich with rain, and the stars are aglow through Thy
gracious providence. This dust-heap of a mortal world
hath been made green and lustrous by Thy bounty, and
the earth hath become an eternal paradise through Thy
mercy, O my God, inasmuch as Thy day of Riḍván hath
arrived, girded with majesty and invested with sovereignty, flooding creation with beams of light like unto
a star, and accompanied by a procession of fervour and
joy. Riḍván hath pitched its tent with dazzling splendour
in the midmost heart of the world, and led its hosts and

sent forth its troops far and wide to the uttermost corners of Paradise.

2 Thus have the hearts of Thy loved ones overflowed with joy and rapture and been carried away in happiness and bliss by Thy sweet savours. They have arisen with yearning and longing to praise Thee, "and drink of a pure beverage shall their Lord shall give them".[18] Praise be to Thee, O my God, for all that Thou hast graciously granted us. Thanks be to Thee, O my Hope, for the bounties Thou hast conferred upon us. Blessings be upon Thee, O my Best-Beloved, for the favours Thou hast chosen to bestow upon us.

3 O God, my God! O Thou Who art the Goal of my desire! Unlock before the faces of Thy loved ones the portals of Thy favours on this perspicuous day. Hoist the sails of guidance above their heads in the Crimson Ark. Cause them to be gathered beneath the standard of Thy bounty and generosity, and send down upon them the sign of Thy grace in the midmost heart of creation. O Lord my God! Make them radiant stars, resplendent lamps, brilliant orbs, and blazing meteors, so that they may arise to serve Thee amongst Thy creatures, kindle the fire of Thy love in the hearts of Thy people, scatter abroad Thy signs throughout Thy realms, and edify the souls of all that dwell on earth. Then shall Thy heavenly repast be outspread throughout the world, this contingent plane become the Abhá Paradise by the power of Thy might, and this nether dust be made the envy of the high heavens through the outpourings of Thy wisdom.

O Lord! Make of Thy loved ones celestial angels 4
who inhabit Thine earth, and enable Thy chosen ones to
become heavenly people who reside in Thy realm. This,
indeed, is the highest aspiration of Thy servant who hath
humbled himself before Thy sovereignty, bowed down in
adoration before Thy door, prostrated himself before Thy
glory, and fallen upon the dust before the power of Thy
sovereign might. Thou art the Bestower, the Compassionate, the Almighty, the All-Bountiful.

O ye spiritual friends of 'Abdu'l-Bahá! At this moment, 5
when the Star of the Riḍván Festival gleameth bright
above the horizon of creation and the whole world is
wrapt in an ecstasy of joy and fervour, it is the time for
rapture and bliss, for exultation and delight, and for the
revelation of this celebrated Day. It is the season to rejoice
and be happy in heart and soul, the time for music and
song, for the melody of harp and lute. The signs of gladness are manifest from every side, and the light of rapture
shineth in all directions. The loved ones of the Lord are
in perfect joy, and His chosen ones beam with delight, for
this is the Day whereon the Most Great Name set out
from the City of God in Iraq and entered the luminous
Garden. On that resplendent Day, the Beloved evinced
such ineffable bliss that the radiance of His joy suffused
the kingdom of existence. On that glorious Day, the Word
of God was exalted amidst all creation.

Wherefore, O ye loved ones of God, it behoveth you 6
all to be filled with such ecstasy and joy on this blessed

Festival as to stir the kingdom of existence into motion. 'Abdu'l-Bahá rejoiceth in these supreme glad-tidings, and supplicateth with the utmost lowliness and fervour at the Threshold of the Abhá Beauty that He may bring gladness to each one of the friends and bestow delight and happiness upon them.

7   It is our hope that, in the year to come, the friends of the All-Merciful who live in free lands will, in a spirit of joy and radiance, lay the foundations of the Mashriqu'l-Adhkár and arise to clearly and openly praise and glorify the Beauty of the Unconstrained and recite the obligatory prayer; for in the realm of worship, fasting and obligatory prayer constitute the two mightiest pillars of God's holy Law. Neglecting them is in no wise permitted, and falling short in their performance is certainly unseemly. In the Tablet of Visitation He saith: "I beseech God, by Thee and by them whose faces have been illumined with the splendours of the light of Thy countenance, and who, for love of Thee, have observed all whereunto they were bidden." He declareth that observance of the commandments of God emanateth from love for the beauty of the Best-Beloved. The seeker, when immersed in the ocean of the love of God, will be moved by intense longing and will arise to carry out the laws of God. Thus, it is impossible for a heart to contain the fragrance of God's love and yet fail to worship the True One, except under conditions when such an action would agitate the enemies and stir up dissension and mischief. Otherwise, a lover of the Abhá

Beauty will no doubt continually demonstrate persever-
ance in the worship of the Lord.

O ye loved ones of God! 'Abdu'l-Bahá is in grave 8
danger by reason of the mischief of the enemies and the
discord fomented by the Centre of Sedition.[19] Whatever
events should come to pass, whether great or small, accuse
ye not a single soul. All such events are due to the revolt
and dissension of the Centre of Sedition. I implore God
to enable him to repent and to return to the Covenant
and the Testament, for otherwise he will, erelong, find
himself in manifest loss. At present, he is considering how
to secure a means of escape, and to flee from the Holy
Land, so that he may engage in further mischief and that,
by his escape, he may cause greater afflictions and troubles
for this servant and for the loved ones of God. He stopped
at nothing and, with all that lay in his power, stirred up
malice, created dissension, spread falsehoods, and dissemi-
nated slander and calumny. All that remaineth for him is
to flee, which, to his disgrace, he is now intent on doing,
thus causing grievous shame and dire turmoil. Should he
find an opportunity, he would not delay his escape even
for a single moment, but it is difficult for him to accom-
plish this plan. However, should this come to pass, the
loved ones of God must be ever watchful and aware, and
must everywhere remain vigilant lest he create a breach
in the Cause of God and spread abroad the foul odours of
enmity. From the Ascension of the Blessed Beauty until
the present day, he hath committed every act that could

harm the Cause of God. Now he is planning this abhorrent and reprehensible act as well.

9   In those days, a few influential notables were planning to procure 'Abdu'l-Bahá's release from confinement. They were fully capable of doing so. But in reply, this servant said, "This citadel is the Prison of the Abhá Beauty. He spent well-nigh four and twenty years here; I have therefore no wish to be released from this prison, nor do I seek deliverance. Nay, rather, I seek renewed confinement and earnestly desire an even more severe incarceration." Those souls were bewildered by my words. But my intent was that they should understand that, in the path of the Lord, prison for us is even as a royal palace, and the depths of the pit as the apex of heaven. This indeed is an unquestionable reality. This verily is the truth, and all else naught but manifest error.

10   The Centre of Sedition cherisheth the hope that once he hath caused the blood of this prisoner to be spilt, he may at last find an arena in which to spur on his charger. Woe unto such idle fancies, such vain imaginings! For lo, some imaginings are a grievous sin. Those who are inebriated with the wine of the Covenant are weary of the stirrers of sedition, and those who seek guidance from the light of Revelation eschew the movers of mischief. Even should the nightingale of faithfulness wing its flight to the garden of eternity, a mindful soul would never give ear unto the croaking of the raven or the cawing of the crow; and even should the comely countenance be concealed

LIGHT OF THE WORLD

behind a veil, no wise person would cast a glance upon an unsightly face. None would ever do so except him who seeketh to stir up sedition or is bereft of reason and discernment. May the Lord shield and protect you from the malice of the ungodly and the mischief of such as have violated His Covenant.

O ye beloved of the Lord! Be united, stand ye together, 11 and cleave tenaciously to the Sure Handle of the Covenant. Bend your energies towards exalting the Word of God, so that the light of Truth may envelop the whole of creation and the darkness of hatred and error may be utterly dispelled.

Were the harm inflicted by the Centre of Sedition 12 directed merely at this servant, and his hatred confined to this wronged prisoner, I swear, by Him besides Whom there is none other God, that I would not have uttered a single word about his scrolls of doubt and his calumnies. But what choice is there? For he hath falsified the words of God, hath sought the ruin of the religion of God, and hath broken the Covenant of God. Had I not tried to awaken the friends by dissipating the doubts through a few words, the Faith of God would have been entirely effaced. I swear by Him besides Whom there is none other God! No choice is left to me but to write these brief words; otherwise, this servant would never have consented to utter a single word of disparagement, even against the fiercest of his foes.

Notwithstanding all that hath passed, I still fervently 13

23

pray and implore God that he may, perchance, leave aside these childish games, turn away from iniquity and rebellion, and repent and enter beneath the shadow of the Covenant. I swear by Him besides Whom there is none other God! I would then show him the utmost love and kindness, would utter not a word about bygone days, and would lay no obligation on him save that he rectify that which he hath falsified in the Sacred Text.

14 Indeed, the very foundation of the Law of God is that His loved ones should consort with all the peoples and kindreds of the earth with the utmost kindliness, fellowship, and unity, and with truthfulness, sincerity, and faithfulness. On no account should they behave towards anyone in a manner contrary to this inviolable principle, save for one who is the embodiment of enmity and is intent upon destroying the Law of God. For such souls, there is no remedy whatsoever. No space should be given them to parade and advance. For otherwise they would bring to naught the glorious martyrdom of the Báb, the shedding of the pure blood of all the martyrs, and the trials, afflictions, and imprisonments suffered by the Luminous Beauty for well-nigh fifty years. They would utterly subvert the mighty foundation of the Cause of God.

15 Therefore, the company of these people should be shunned and none should associate with them, unless they repent unto God. My Lord is verily the Compassionate, the Forgiving. Such repentance, however, must be sincere

and not merely in words. The repentance of the Centre of Sedition would consist in his rectifying all that he hath interpolated in the Text, confessing to that which he hath done, and imploring God's pardon and forgiveness. For, one day, he came to see 'Abdu'l-Bahá through the intercession of 'Alí-Akbar. He shut the door, confessed his transgressions, and asked forgiveness for his trespasses. This servant did indeed forgive him, but after a few days it became clear and evident that this too had been but one of his deceitful designs. His true intention had been to meet certain persons in private and sow the seeds of doubt in their hearts, for the friends had been shunning his company. The point is that true repentance must be distinguished from false. Only then can it be accepted. Upon you be greetings and praise.

7

He is God.

O servant of Bahá! Thy detailed letters have been suc- 1
cessively received, and despite the lack of a single free moment, they have all been read with the utmost attention. Consider with how many thousands of souls such correspondence must be maintained, and how difficult is the task; there is no time at all. Therefore, a brief reply is being written, which thou wilt surely excuse. I

write thee by reason of my love for thee; otherwise, the writing of even a single word would be impossible.

2   Teaching the Cause in this day is the head cornerstone of the foundation itself. Whosoever ariseth to teach shall be graciously aided by the hosts of the celestial Concourse. Naught else will lead to any success whatsoever. Today is the day for laying the foundation, not the time for organization, repair, or restoration. One must first lay the foundation, and only then organize and arrange.

3   Laying the foundation consisteth solely in the propagation of the Faith of God, in the diffusion of the divine fragrances, and in detachment from all else but Him. Consider how a skilled builder first procureth the necessary materials for the edifice. He then prepareth the groundwork, layeth the foundation, and raiseth the pillars. Only afterwards doth he attend to its organization, arrangement, and adornment. Were we to concentrate on organization and arrangement at this time, the teaching of the Cause of God and the diffusion of the divine fragrances would be delayed.

4   Therefore, be thou occupied with naught but the promotion of the Cause in the environs of Shíráz. If the people of a city, of their own accord, choose to hold a consultative gathering—that is, to form a Spiritual Assembly according to the electoral process—well and good. However, we should not be actively pursuing this matter at present, for then some would be pleased, while others would be saddened, and still others distressed.

Such decisions are to be left to the believers in each city. 'Abdu'l-Bahá, and all who join him and have a share in his servitude at the Sacred Threshold, should centre their thoughts on spreading the sweet savours of God. Had 'Abdu'l-Bahá occupied himself with those other matters, how could he have illumined the East and the West with the light of guidance?

Thy questions will be briefly answered. The Ancient 5 Beauty[20]—may my life be offered up for His loved ones— did not to outward seeming meet His Holiness, the Exalted One[21]—may my life be a sacrifice unto Him.

The Faithful Spirit, Gabriel, the Holy Spirit, and the 6 One mighty in power are all designations of the same Reality.

The elected members of Spiritual Assemblies must 7 needs be pure and sanctified. Whenever a Spiritual Assembly is formed in a city, it behoveth the teachers of the Cause to consult with it and to act according to whatsoever it deemeth advisable. The teacher should not lay hands on worldly things, whether pertaining to contributions or the like. Should the people in a locality elect a teacher as a member of the Spiritual Assembly, this is permissible....

To conclude, O Jináb-i-Shukúhí, be thou severed 8 from all save God and enraptured by the fragrances of the Divine. Forsaking home and comfort, become a wanderer, roaming the wilderness of the love of God and engaged in the diffusion of His sweet savours. If thou seekest divine assistance, this is the way; if thou yearnest

for confirmations, this is the path. By the Ancient Beauty!
All else save this will eventually result in manifest loss.
This, verily, is the truth, and all else naught but error.

8

He is the Most Glorious.

¹ O thou distinguished branch of the blessed and sacred
Lote-Tree! When the Ancient Beauty, the Most
Great Name—may my life be offered up for His loved
ones—would visit Haifa, He would time and again praise
a certain spot on Mount Carmel, saying what a pleasant
and agreeable place it was and what a splendid view it
offered. He instructed that it be purchased by whatever
means possible. He was most intent on acquiring that site.

² Four years ago, with great effort, that land was purchased, and following some minor preparations, it was
made ready. Special instructions were then conveyed to
Rangoon, numerous epistles written, and a design prepared and sent, for a sarcophagus to be made of the marble of that region. The carving made from a single piece
of stone was completed with great difficulty, and the sarcophagus was transported here by various means. Thou
hast surely heard of what transpired along the way, when
it entered certain cities. In short, it arrived not long ago,
together with a casket made of the finest Indian wood.

A year ago, we dispatched Áqá Mírzá Asadu'lláh from ₃
here on a specific mission. So it was that he and a few
of the friends transported, upon a palanquin and with
the utmost reverence, lowliness, humility, and respect, that
holy Temple and mighty Throne, the sacred remains of
the Báb—may my life be sacrificed for His dust—from
Persia to the Holy Land.

We are now engaged in raising this sacred edifice on ₄
Mount Carmel. God willing, we will also summon thee
to join us and take part in carrying the stones and mortar
of this hallowed and blessed Shrine, that thou mayest partake of the limitless effusions of His grace and attain this
most mighty honour. These are tidings of joy with which
the sovereignty of heaven and earth cannot compare. In
truth, my heart is filled with such great joy and gladness as
cannot be described. For that sacred Temple had suffered
great indignity at the hands of the transgressors, but now,
praise be to God, through the unfailing help and grace
vouchsafed by the Ancient Beauty, all the means have
been procured and arranged so perfectly as shall cause
everyone to marvel. The glory of God rest upon thee and
upon the Afnán of the sacred Tree in that land.

9

1   O thou seeker of truth! Thy letter was received. Thou hast asked me for a written history as well as a record of the prophecies concerning the Báb and Bahá'u'lláh. These have both been previously written. Search for them and thou wilt find them.

2   Regarding the Blessed Beauty, He was not born of the line of Ishmael but was, rather, a descendant of one of the other brothers who had migrated to Persia and the Afghan territories. For, apart from Isaac and Ishmael, Abraham had six sons who all moved to Persia and to the Afghan regions.

3   O thou sincere seeker! Strive thou with all thy might to summon the people to the heavenly Kingdom, so that through divine guidance thou mayest enable the human souls to become even as the angels of Paradise, mayest promote universal peace in this distinguished Age and serve the oneness of the world of humanity, and mayest attain unto everlasting life, follow the example of Christ, and become a companion of 'Abdu'l-Bahá in this path. Upon thee be greetings and praise.

10

1   O thou noble branch of the divine Tree! Countless occupations and endless vicissitudes have delayed my reply to thy letter. This thou wilt surely forgive, inasmuch

as my obligations are such as cannot be described or expressed. Notwithstanding this, praise be to God, communications between 'Abdu'l-Bahá and the honourable Twigs of the Sacred Tree are continuous.[22] This is because of the deep love I cherish in my heart for the Exalted Beauty—may my life be offered up for Him.

God be praised, the construction of the lower level of 2 the Holy Shrine, in utmost strength, grace, and elegance, hath been completed. There was a large plot of land located on the slope above the Holy Shrine. Had it remained in the hands of strangers, they might have constructed buildings there in the future, leading to great difficulties. Time and again, that ground was blessed by the footsteps of Bahá'u'lláh. There were a few cypress trees therein, and the Blessed Beauty—may my life be offered up for His loved ones—frequently sat under their shade while the believers attained His presence. That land also had to be purchased recently for the sum of two thousand túmáns, and was conjoined with the precincts of the Holy Shrine.

As to the cistern,[23] since this servant was imprisoned 3 before its construction, the European and Ottoman engineers proved unequal to the task of ensuring the required soundness and solidity of the structure, and their work was left incomplete. Consequently the cistern wall facing the sea collapsed, and the efforts were somewhat wasted. However, no harm was done, for it is now being reconstructed most solidly, under the supervision of this servant, and will soon be completed. Although due to my incarceration I have been unable to go to the Holy Shrine in person, I have been supervising the construction work from a distance. It will soon be complete and will be most firm and solid. Indeed, it is not a cistern, but a sea!

4   And now concerning the visit of the holy leaf of the Blessed Tree: God willing, circumstances will soon make this advisable, and permission will then be granted. Upon thee be greetings and praise.

II

He is God.

1   O thou my fellow countryman! Although 'Abdu'l-Bahá was born in Ṭihrán and for successive years wandered homeless in Iraq, and although he was for a time an exile in Rumelia and for forty years a prisoner in 'Akká, yet his homeland is Mázindarán—that is to say, the district of Míyánrúd in the region of Núr. Therefore, I address thee as my countryman.

2   Thy splendid letter aroused spiritual affections in my heart. I read it with admiration, for it was a melody of Divine Unity and an ensign proclaiming His oneness. I, too, am most eager to meet thee. If the means become available for thee to travel in peace and tranquillity, thou mayest come next winter.

3   Praised be God! Whenever I read the name of someone

from Mázindarán at the end of any letter, it bringeth me gladness and delight, inasmuch as it is the ancestral home of the family of the Blessed Beauty. My heart longeth for that land to become even as Paradise itself, and for its people to recognize and embrace the Great Announcement. The Glory of Glories rest upon thee.

12

He is God.

O sorely tried friends of 'Abdu'l-Bahá! It hath become [1] apparent that a wicked person in those regions hath assailed and attacked both rich and poor, hath harmed and harassed friend and foe alike. He hath pillaged and plundered many, robbed and levied taxes on all. Not a soul did he spare; not a single penny did he let remain. This indeed was a dire calamity, a most great affliction, for it wreaked woeful loss and inflicted boundless hardship upon friend and stranger alike.

Had he not acted so, he might not have become afflicted [2] with the retribution which such behaviour entaileth. The day will soon come when he shall fall into distress and be brought to naught. Neither name nor fame shall remain of him. All this mischief, however, may be blamed on the sinister schemes and transgressions of outdated Signs; this thunderbolt was cast as a result of the decrees pronounced by defective Proofs.[24] And yet, a band of witless ones still follow after such men, still kiss their hands and the hem of their garments, and are scorched by the flames of mischief and sedition.

3   In brief, let not the loved ones of God be grieved or distressed at these countless afflictions, for in bearing such trials they share in the sufferings of the Abhá Beauty. Although that radiant Luminary was merciful, loving, and forgiving to all, the ignorant kindled such fires that they burned away all sense of decency and shame. As a result, that focal Centre of beauty was subjected to chains and fetters; He endured the bastinado and was afflicted, day and night, with all manner of torture. He was made homeless and a wanderer in mountains and plains; He was banished, exiled, and imprisoned. He spent twenty-five long years in confinement and was insulted and tormented. Let the friends render thanks unto God, therefore, that they too have suffered pillage and plunder, that they too have been targeted by the darts of cruelty and malice.

4   The village of the Blessed Beauty in Mázindarán was attacked by a host of twelve thousand brutal men. They plundered and pillaged so relentlessly that no sign of any possession or goods remained; they even left no crop for the inhabitants of the village. They set fire to the straw, burned the oil, and massacred a number of the innocent. They then herded the peasants together in chains, sent them to Ṭihrán, and cast them into prison. They cut the chin as well as the beard of that spirit of spirits, Mullá

34

'Abdu'l-Fattáḥ, and they marched him to Ṭihrán, barefoot and in chains. Despite his old age and his frailty, the guards showed him no mercy. But even whilst bound by chains and on foot, with blood pouring from his wounded face, that spirit of detachment raised up his voice in prayer, to his very last breath, rendering thanks unto the Lord of Signs for having been made the victim of plunder and pillage, for having been bound in shackles and fetters in the path of the Beloved. With his beard tinged with his own blood, he walked all the way and, upon arrival at the prison in Ṭihrán, surrendered his soul into the hands of his Beloved and sacrificed himself for the Loving Friend. Beaming with joy, he laid down his life in the path of that great Luminary. How truly hath the poet said:

> That beam of bliss and ecstasy
> Did stay with him forevermore,
> Even as Aḥmad, the Praised,
> Who is always with the Peerless Lord.

In short, let the loved ones of God render thanks 5 unto the All-Merciful Lord for their share of these afflictions and for their astounding patience and forbearance. Through His unfailing grace, a radiant morn shall surely follow this dreary night, and a bright horizon will succeed this foul cloud. This deadly poison shall give way to purest honey, and this sore wound will at last receive a healing balm. The Glory of Glories rest upon you!

13

He is God.

1 O servant of the Abhá Beauty! Thy letter was received. Thou hast written of being deprived of communications for some time, whereas I have sent forth numerous letters. I also penned one to the handmaiden of Bahá regarding the Shrine of the Báb, and about how on the day of Naw-Rúz the sacred Remains were deposited, with the utmost joy and radiance, within the marble casket and placed, with due grace and ceremony, in the exalted Shrine. The receipt of that letter was also not confirmed. But thy letter giving the joyful tidings of the holding of a gathering was received on the first day of Riḍván and rejoiced my heart.

2 Thou hast enquired regarding a certain passage from the Epistle addressed to the Wolf. "The Land of Mím" referreth to Mázindarán. The Blessed Beauty was confined to prison in the town of Ámul, and, as the 'ulamá gathered together in the mosque, He was delivered into their hands. Those iniquitous divines then rose up against Him with injustice and tyranny. They afflicted Him with a myriad torments and made Him the victim of their relentless cruelty. For instance, they subjected the Blessed Beauty to the bastinado in such wise that His feet were sore wounded for some time. Convey my loving greetings to the maid-servant of Bahá, as well as to the rest of the friends.

14

He is God.

O thou remnant of those two distinguished departed 1
souls! Thy letter was received and brought infinite
joy and gladness; for, the Lord be praised, news hath come
at last from the land of Núr, and a letter hath arrived from
a soul who is a descendant of veteran friends and dearly
loved countrymen.

Glorified be God! The East is illumined with the splen- 2
dours of His light, and the West is perfumed with the sweet
savours of the love of the Lord. The Turks and the Persians,
the Africans and the Americans, the Europeans and the
Asians have all been set aflame and made vibrant through
the pervading influence of the Cause of God. Yet the
homeland of the Blessed Beauty, though bearing the name
of Núr,[25] hath remained darksome and deprived. Strangers have become friends, whilst those who were friends
are estranged. Balál the Ethiopian, Ṣuhayb the Byzantine,
'Addás the Assyrian, and Salmán the Persian were all made
intimates of the mysteries. And yet the Siyyid of Quraysh,
Abú-Lahab, as well as the kinsmen and relatives of the
Beauteous Muḥammad, remained bereft of the splendour
of His Light.

In the Gospel it is said that all the prophets have been 3
without honour in their own country and homeland.
Indeed, such is the case. Christ hath likewise said that

37

many shall come from the East and from the West and enter the kingdom of heaven, whilst the children of the kingdom shall forsake it. And now, the fame of the Cause of God and the tidings of the advent of Bahá'u'lláh have stirred up and set in motion all the regions of the earth. Yet the people of the district of Núr remain deprived. Take then good heed, O ye people of insight!

4   While returning from Mázindarán to Ṭihrán, the Blessed Beauty passed through Núr, filling Tákur and Dárkulá with enthusiasm and ecstasy. A great multitude became His faithful followers, and their numbers increased from day to day.... In brief, a vast number were attracted to the holy fragrances of God.

5   A year later, Yaḥyá the unchaste proceeded to Núr.[26] In hardly any time at all, he provoked agitation and great confusion there, and when at last he found himself in trouble, and saw the likelihood of being in danger in that region, he abandoned the faithful friends and left. In the guise of a dervish, he escaped to Gílán, Mázindarán, and Kirmánsháh, leaving all those helpless souls to be massacred. He bolted, fled, and vanished in retreat. He ensnared the friends, most of whom were martyred. The situation he created in that village, the way he behaved, caused the fire of the love of God to be utterly extinguished therein. He even prompted a few to attack the late Mírzá Khudávirdí. I remember, as a child in Núr, seeing Mírzá Khudávirdí sobbing aloud and saying, "For fifty years I have served this family; was it justified that Mírzá Yaḥyá should incite Gul-Bábá to beat

me publicly, to insult me, and to turn me away?" Briefly, as a result of his evil deeds, the light of Núr was obscured and Míyánrúd fell into a state of torpor.

One day, in an assemblage in Dárkulá, the Blessed 6 Beauty spoke in such an eloquent manner and presented such powerful proofs and testimonies that, when He arose to depart, four of the mujtahids rushed forth to bring Him His shoes. Two of those were Mullá 'Abbás and Mullá Abu'l-Qásim, sons-in-law of Mírzá Muḥammad-Taqíy-i-Mujtahid. That was the condition aforetime, and this is what hath befallen since.

15

He is God.

O servant of God! Ṭihrán is the homeland of the 1 compassionate Beloved and the abode of that Light of the realms of the Placeless. Thou too hast been planted by the hand of celestial power in that same garden and been nurtured by the gentle breezes and pleasing waters of that luminous land. Wherefore, even as outwardly thou art from the homeland of that resplendent Light, it is my hope that also inwardly thou mayest become a denizen of the heavenly Kingdom of that shining Orb.

If thou art debarred from the public baths, praised be 2 God, for thou art immersed instead in that wellspring of cool water that is "to wash with and to drink",[27] and art indeed a sorely tried and true believer in the path of the Blessed Beauty. Upon thee be greetings and praise.

16

He is God.

1   O Bashír-i-Iláhí! Thy letter was like unto a treasury of poems in glorification and praise of the Blessed Beauty. It hath imparted the utmost joy and gladness. Each word of thy letter is a sign of joyous music: One word is the lyre and the lute; another, the psalms of the House of David. One word is the timbrel and the harp; another, pure poetry and song. It is a perfect symphony, causing the listeners to leap with rapture and joy. From afar thou playest the melody, and here His lovers rejoice with ecstasy.

2   Praise be to God, for thy letter was redolent with the fragrance of musk and thy words were as sweet as honey. It bore testimony to the unity and harmony among the friends, who are one and all engaged, with zeal and attraction, unity and concord, in exalting the Word of God, diffusing His fragrances, and teaching His Cause, none burdened by sorrow.

3   The four pages in the blessed handwriting of the Báb— may my life be a sacrifice unto Him—that thou didst present to 'Abdu'l-Bahá as a gift were received. Thereupon,

the very walls resounded with the anthem of "O blessed, blessed are we!" whilst 'Abdu'l-Bahá hearkened from a corner unto these sweet melodies. Well done! Well done, for having cheered our hearts with such a cherished gift.

As to thy stay in the Murgh-Mahallih of Shimírán for 4 a change of air, this is truly a divine favour.[28] That place is not the abode of mere birds, but the nest of the Phoenix of the East and the dwelling of the mystic Bird of the sacred Mount. For there, in that pure and hallowed field, the Blessed Beauty—may my life be offered up for His loved ones—took up residence for an entire summer. There he resided in the garden of Ḥájí-Báqir, which consisted of three terraces overlooking a lake. This was in the earliest days of the Cause, when that district became the throne of the Lord of the Kingdom. A large stone platform was raised in the heart of the lake, with a tent in the centre and gardens all around. About one hundred and fifty friends would gather, and at night hymns of praise would rise up to the Concourse on high. Those were wonderful times indeed. The Blessed Beauty would frequently make mention of that place.

And now, render thou thanks unto God for having 5 bestowed such a dwelling upon thee, where thou hast engaged, in the company of the friends, in praise and remembrance of the incomparable Lord, singing to thy heart's content and bringing bliss and joy to His loved ones. The Glory of Glories rest upon thee.

17

He is God.

1 O handmaid of Bahá! Thy letter was received, and from its contents the earnestness with which thou art serving the Abhá Kingdom became evident. Thou art indeed striving with heart and soul, and I am well pleased with thee.

2 I had the book thou hast written about Qurratu'l-'Ayn rendered into Arabic.[29] The translation is exceedingly eloquent; I have read through it carefully. If necessary, I can forward a copy of the Arabic to thee.

3 With regard to the episode of Bada<u>sh</u>t, though the account is accurate, it is not exhaustive. A fuller description would be that Qurratu'l-'Ayn was in one garden and Quddús in another, whilst the Blessed Beauty resided in a tent. His tent was raised between the two gardens, beside a stream. The Blessed Beauty had previously said unto Quddús and Qurratu'l-'Ayn that the Cause was to be fully proclaimed. The next day, He fell ill. Quddús entered and sat in the presence of the Blessed Beauty, with all the believers gathered round the tent. Suddenly, Qurratu'l-'Ayn emerged from her garden and, roaring and crying out, she entered the tent and seated herself. "Read the Súrih of the Event", the Blessed Beauty proclaimed, and it was read in His presence. The greatest commotion then came to pass: Some fled, others wept and cried aloud, and

yet others were sorely perturbed. Mullá Ismá'íl cut his own throat, and the gathering at Bada<u>sh</u>t was dispersed.

In short, thou hast indeed been most assiduous in writing this book. I beseech God that as day followeth day, thy spirit of endeavour, service, and sacrifice, and thy constancy and steadfastness in the Cause, may wax stronger so that thou mayest become a luminous star shining from the horizon of eternity. 4

Dispatch some copies of this book by post to Persia for the friends, but do so one volume at a time, for should ye send several copies at once, the government will confiscate them.... 5

18

He is God.

O 'Abdu'l-Vahháb! During His first journey to Iraq, the Blessed Beauty met a young man by the name of Mírzá 'Abdu'l-Vahháb. No sooner had this youth attained His presence and hearkened unto His words than, lo, he became so magnetized, so suffused with joy, that he guided his family to the truth and imparted the gladsome tidings to a great many. 1

Following the return of Him Who is the Most Great Name to Ṭihrán, Mírzá 'Abdu'l-Vahháb hastened to that sacred land, dancing with delight and leaping with joy, 2 only to be consigned, upon arrival, to the depths of the dungeon. A few days later, his turn came to be martyred. When the executioner stepped into the dungeon and shouted out his name, that young man, still in the prime of his years, leapt to his feet, danced for joy in that prison, and surrendered himself to the executioner. Thus did he attain supreme martyrdom. The Blessed Beauty frequently spoke of him. I fervently hope that the joy and radiance of that 'Abdu'l-Vahháb may also be manifested in this one. The Glory of Glories rest upon thee.

19

He is God.

1   O thou who art steadfast in the Covenant! Thou hast asked concerning the travels of Bahá'u'lláh. The Blessed Beauty—may my life be offered up for His loved ones—travelled directly from Ṭihrán to Hamadán, from that city to Kirmánsháh, and thence straight on to Baghdad.

2   As regardeth the association which hath been formed in Shanghai, China, with the aim of promoting harmony and reconciliation amongst the religions, do thou send to that English lady literature about the Cause and material from the press, and advise her by all means to go to that association and speak about this blessed Cause—a universal religion which bringeth all faiths and creeds together

beneath the effulgence of the Sun of Truth, entirely reconciling them and welding them into a single people. This is an important matter to which thou shouldst attend most heedfully. Correspond regularly with them and, if it be possible, send teachers to those parts, who may likewise go to the association and spread the divine teachings. Only such souls should be sent, however, as are detached from the world, attracted by the fragrances of holiness, and distinguished by the utmost purity and sanctity.

20

He is the All-Glorious.

O thou servant of the Sacred Threshold! Thy letter [1] dated 23 May 1921 was received and its contents were noted. The complaints of the two parties are continuous, and their tale-telling also incessant. This causeth grief to 'Abdu'l-Bahá, who had painstakingly arranged for thy return to the sacred House, thereby delivering the friends from deep anguish and despair, and cheering their hearts with joy! Now, differences have arisen and will no doubt lead to the House being lost to us once again.

In short, O servant of the Sacred Threshold! 'Abdu'l- [2] Bahá hath set upon thy head a gem-studded crown, which is the custodianship of the sacred House. Its full significance is not as yet evident, but erelong it will acquire great importance. This crown shall suffice thee and a hundred generations after thee. Entangle not thyself, then, in other affairs.

3 Seek, with the utmost tranquillity and composure, to dedicate thyself to service at the sacred House, and treat the pilgrims with the utmost kindliness and love, so that they may be happy and pleased with thee. There is nothing greater than such servitude to the sacred House; thou couldst not wish for more. In short, strive with heart and soul to please and satisfy all the friends.

4 Thou hast seen the conduct and behaviour of 'Abdu'l-Bahá. Follow this example. Act in accordance with the admonitions of the Blessed Beauty—may my life be offered up for His loved ones. That Wronged One of the world consorted with all people with the utmost meekness and humility. Throughout the long period when He resided in Baghdad, not a single heart was saddened by Him. All the inhabitants of that city were thankful and obliged to Him.

5 Thus we, who are the servants of His threshold, must follow in His blessed footsteps. This, indeed, is the means of success. This, indeed, is the cause of prosperity. Convey my wholehearted greetings to thy brothers and thy relatives. The Glory of Glories rest upon thee.

21

He is God.

O thou who art steadfast in the Covenant! The letter 1 thou hadst written to Mashhadí Ismá'íl hath been received. The traces of the pen of that loving friend have brought joy to my heart and mind, for their inner meanings are spiritual impressions and heartfelt sentiments derived from the reality of the soul; they are sufficient testimony to firmness and constancy, and to servitude to the all-sufficing Lord.

From the earliest dawn of the Morn of divine guidance, 2 Ádhirbáyján raised aloft the banner of faith and certitude, and the Cause of God thereby spread far and wide. But following the martyrdom of the Exalted One, the journey of the Blessed Beauty from Iraq to Kurdistan, and the seclusion of Yaḥyá in a corner of oblivion, the Cause of God sank deep into apathy everywhere, even in Ádhirbáyján. Only a few souls remained steadfast and calm until the Day-Star of the world returned to Iraq and the splendours of His light shone upon all regions in the plenitude of their glory. Once again, a Great Resurrection was witnessed and the sweet savours of holiness were shed upon the whole world. The friends in Ádhirbáyján were stirred up in blissful rapture, and their enthusiasm, joy, and fervour waxed greater day by day.

Now, too, receptivity in that land is great, but a mighty 3

47

effort is needed if the friends are to impart these joyful tidings with gladness and delight, and to perfume the senses of the seekers with the fragrance of the robe of the divine Joseph. Praise be to God that thou hast arisen to serve Him and art earnestly striving to exalt the Word of God. My hope is that, through the sincerity of souls, the hearts and minds of the people of Ádhirbáyján may be stirred in these days, and sanctified beings may arise to guide the people aright. The forces of the Kingdom stand ready and expectant. As soon as a soul urgeth the steed of high endeavour into the field of sacrifice, these heavenly forces will rush forth to his aid and will render him assistance and support.

4   Thou hadst requested permission for a visit. At this time, thy presence in those regions is much needed. Thou art occupied with service, manifesting complete servitude and devoted to the promotion of the Word of God. Such service is the same as attaining to the Sacred Threshold of the Lord. The Glory of Glories rest upon thee.

22

1   O Lord, my God! Thou seest how the son of Maḥmúd hath been seized with trembling and dismay, at the hand of hostile enemies.[30] The vast immensity of the world was for him straitened, inasmuch as multiple calamities befell him and adversities waxed increasingly severe. He was so overtaken by the darkness of tyranny and

injustice, of cruelty and iniquity, that, unable to endure the onslaught of those trials and tribulations, he finally forsook hearth and home and migrated to the Holy Land.

O God! Persia hath become the arena for the hosts of 2 woe and tyranny. Animosity amongst contending groups hath fanned the flames of injustice and rebellion throughout that land. None can be found there whose breast is not pierced by arrows, whose heart is not wounded by spears. None is there whose body hath not fallen upon the dust-heap of infamy and degradation, owing to the growing intensity of contention and strife and by reason of what the hands of the evil plotters have wrought. Some lean to the right, others turn back on their heels; still others bring upon themselves abasement and retribution. The people have become divided and the congregation of those who were wrapt in veils dispersed, inasmuch as they have failed to hearken to His decisive decree and, deaf to counsel, have cast themselves into the depths of the sea of doubt.

O Lord! Tribulations have encompassed all the peoples. 3 There is none to dispel them besides Thee, and none to forgive our sins except Thyself. I beseech Thee to shield Thy loved ones and protect Thy chosen ones from the swirling dust that hath encompassed that land. I implore Thee, in particular, to shield this devoted servant of Thine, Ja'far, who hath been praying fervently to Thee and supplicating in tears before Thy Face. He is destitute and hath placed his complete trust and confidence in Thee.

O Lord! Relieve him of his ills, and let him not drown in the deepest abyss of tribulations or in the fathomless ocean of afflictions. Bestow upon him Thy manifold bounties, unravel before him Thy hidden mysteries, and preserve him from every affliction and sorrow, within the stronghold of Thine unfailing protection. O God! Open Thou the gates of joy and happiness for him in this marvellous age, so that the verities of Thy Cause may flow from him in torrents to every ardent and grateful soul. O Lord! Grant that his sole aim, his only goal, may be to diffuse Thy sweet savours amidst humankind and to spread Thy light throughout the world. O Thou my compassionate Lord! Thou art, in truth, the God of bounty, the Almighty, the All-Glorious, the Ever-Forgiving.

4   O thou dear friend! Thy letter, filled with sighs of grief, was read with the utmost sorrow. Thou hast indeed fallen into grave difficulties and hast endured extreme hardships. But this year of great calamity hath encompassed all of Persia—nay, it hath enveloped the whole world. As attested by the poet, "No thorn is there that is not crimsoned by the martyrs' blood."[31]

5   'Abdu'l-Bahá hath also been thy partner and associate in this regard. In Paris, while, on the one hand, each noble soul brought joy to our hearts, on the other, great difficulties arose as a result of attacks by small-minded individuals. In London some of the clergy hurled such assaults upon us as are impossible to describe. Wert thou to read the *Churchman*, thou wouldst know what things have come

to pass.[32] But 'Abdu'l-Bahá payeth no heed whatsoever to any ordeal, difficulty, or adversity. Nay, rather, he regardeth adversity to be, at times, the same as bounty itself. For forty years the prison-city of 'Akká was for him a heavenly paradise, and he saw the early days of that imprisonment, which were its most severe, as a garden of roses.

Thou too must be my companion, and abandon not 6 the arena in the face of afflictions and calamities. Thou must not merely refrain from complaining, but must rather be thankful. One day in Baghdad, the Blessed Beauty—may my soul be offered up for His servants—addressing us, uttered this verse:

Either speak no more of love, or content thyself
    with what hath been ordained;
Thus hath it been decreed by My command, and
    such is My law and My way.[33]

At that instant, 'Abdu'l-Bahá understood what was expected of him.

And now, through His infinite favours, I hope that days 7 as sweet as honey may once again return. Grieve not, neither sorrow nor repine. "Forsake all complaint and tend to the flock."[34] My wish for thee is that, by the favour of the Blessed Beauty, thou mayest find ease of heart and soul. The Glory of Glories rest upon thee.

23

He is the All-Glorious.

1   O thou who hast tasted of the sweetness of every affliction in the path of God, who hast arisen with thy spirit, thy being, and thine inmost essence to serve His Cause and to exalt His Word! Upon thee rest the glory of God, the All-Glorious.

2   A few days ago, Áqá Siyyid Muḥammad-Riḍá, a resident of Mázindarán, together with Mullá Ramaḍán—upon them be the glory of God, the All-Glorious—and another person arrived and visited the blessed Shrine. Since then, we have been meeting day and night.

3   One day, during the time in Iraq, the Ancient Beauty—may my spirit, my being, and mine essence be offered up for the earth ennobled by the footsteps of His loved ones—said: "Since Fárs is the homeland of the Exalted One—the Primal Point—and is associated with that Holy Being, I deeply yearn for it to be set ablaze with the fire of the love of God." Shortly thereafter, the Báb's maternal uncle, the honourable Afnán, arrived, attained His presence, and submitted some questions. The Epistle to the Uncle, titled the "Kitáb-i-Íqán", was thus revealed. The province of Fárs was then set aflame with the love of God, and the light of knowledge dawned forth and shone resplendent from that horizon. Many souls entered beneath the shadow of the Word of God, and some, filled with the holy ecstasy of His

bounty, hastened to the field of sacrifice and flung away their lives and hearts.

Now, it is clear and evident from these words of 4 Bahá'u'lláh what must be His irresistible will and desire for the province of Mázindarán. I swear by His holy Being! The Concourse on high and the denizens of the Abhá Kingdom are expectantly awaiting the time when, in that blessed region which is associated with the Ancient Beauty—may my life be offered up for His loved ones— the ocean of God's love will surge and swell forthwith; the flame of the fire kindled in the Burning Bush will ignite every tree, whether green or sere; souls will be raised up who, even as resplendent stars, will illuminate the celestial firmament; and realities will appear who, like unto manifest signs and upraised banners, will exalt the Word of God.

Therefore it behoveth thee to ponder so inestimable 5 a benefit and to seize every means within thy power, that perchance thou mayest manifest God's irrevocable purpose, exert thyself anew, and render a wondrous service to His Cause. The glory of God rest upon thee.

24

He is God.

O ye who yearn for the beauty of the compassionate Beloved! No sooner had He Who is the Beloved of the worlds, the Desire of the spiritually minded, the Object of the adoration of the heavenly souls, and the Promised One of the people of the Bayán been made manifest in Iraq than He stirred and quickened the earth, and shed His radiant light upon human conduct and character. The universe was set in motion, and the whole creation was filled with joy. The reality of each created thing acquired its heavenly significance, and every atom in existence attained unto the Divine Beloved. The East became the Dawning-Place of splendours, and the West was made the horizon of effulgent glory. The earth became heavenly, and darksome dust was made radiant. The glory of the Kingdom was revealed in the world of creation, and this nether realm was awakened to the Realm on high. This world became another world, and the realm of being acquired a new life.

With every passing day, these signs will be revealed and made more manifest, these lights will shine more resplendent; and with every passing moment, this musk-laden breeze will shed its perfume upon the world. But alas! The people of Persia remain wrapt in heedless slumber and, like the blind and the deaf, neither see the Light nor hear the Call. They are neither awakened nor mindful.

Strive then and exert a mighty effort, for Persia is 3 the homeland of the compassionate Beloved, and Fárs the dawning-place of the resplendent Morn. Perchance, through the high endeavours of the friends, the inhabitants of that land may perceive the rays of that luminous Orb, and may receive their portion of manifold grace from the Lord of tokens and signs. The Glory of Glories rest upon you!

25

He is God.

O ye who stand fast and firm in the Covenant! No 1 sooner had the Most Great Luminary of the world risen above the horizon of Iraq and shed its radiance upon all regions from the Source of divine glory, than all the bats of darkness, with their pomp and pride, assailed it from every side, that they might conceal that manifest Light from the eyes of His favoured ones and soar to prominence under cover of darkness in the gloom of night. Since their arguments proved powerless against Him, they devised schemes for the departure of the Blessed Beauty. They resorted to innumerable machinations, so that the Day-Star of the world might sink below the horizon of

Iraq and the Light of sanctity might be prevented from shining forth from the heights of Divine Unity. And so it came to pass that they conducted the Blessed Beauty from the East to the West.

2   But this exile and isolation became the means for the exaltation of the Word of God and led to the diffusion of the divine fragrances. The Eagle of His Cause soared unto the summits of grandeur, and the Day-Star of His Word shone forth from the horizon of might and power. This abasement became a source of confirmation, this remoteness a means of reunion. The vitality of God's Faith was strengthened, and its fame was noised abroad. The Faith was already renowned in Persia, but this exile caused the whole earth to resound with its praise and its reputation to spread throughout the world.

3   Though this should have served as a lesson, it led to more heedlessness among the ignorant. Soon afterwards, they once again hoisted the banners of hatred, sowed the seeds of malice in the hearts, and incited certain foes to oppose Him. They found a means and an instrument in the person of Mírzá Yaḥyá, the nominee of the Báb. His Excellency the Ambassador used this undiscerning individual as his chief instrument for stirring up mischief.[35] Mírzá Yaḥyá had fondly imagined that if the Lamp of the Realm of Glory could be removed from its niche in the West, this new Cause and its flood of abounding grace would be reduced to naught. He therefore joined forces with the Ambassador and began, both overtly and covertly,

to stir up a myriad storms of mischief and sedition. He imagined that this harm would befall the Ancient Beauty, and that such malice would injure His blessed Person, while he himself would remain safe and secure. How far, how very far otherwise it proved to be! When the fire of dissension blazed high, that ignorant one was exiled even before the departure of the Beauty of the All-Merciful, and he remaineth to this very day lamenting in the abyss of disappointment and loss.

However, when that resplendent Sun rose above the 4 horizon of His prison, the light of His sanctity was shed over the Holy Land, God's burning Fire burst into mighty flames, and the heat of His love blazed fiercely in the midmost heart of the world. The all-embracing reality of the Word of God rose from the nadir to the most exalted zenith, and the mystery of these words was made manifest: "Fain would they put out God's light with their mouths: But God hath willed to perfect His light, albeit the infidels abhor it."[36] How well hath the poet said: "Even a foe can become the source of good, were this to be the Lord's desire."

Behold the greatness of God's inscrutable wisdom. 5 Some three thousand years ago, He imparted through the tongue of the Prophets glad-tidings unto the Holy Land in words such as these: Rejoice, O Holy Land, for thou shalt be made the footstool of the All-Merciful! The Tabernacle of the Lord shall be raised, the sweet savours of holiness shall be diffused, and the Day-Star of holiness shall shine forth.

Rejoice with exceeding gladness, O Holy Land, rejoice! That bright Moon shall beam forth in thy heaven, and that glorious Sun shall shine resplendent from thine Orient.[37]

6   He Who is the Desire of the World wished, through His consummate wisdom, to fulfil the promises of the Prophets uttered some two or three thousand years ago. He roused up His enemies and made them the instruments of His all-swaying power, so that they might uproot their foundations with their own hands and banish this resplendent Light from the niche of its native land, that thereby its radiance might shine upon the Holy Land and the promises of the Prophets be fulfilled, this sacred vale might be made the gathering place of the friends of God and these hallowed precincts become the focal centre of the celestial arena, and the light of Divine Unity might shine forth and the darkness of ignorance be dispelled. This, verily, proceedeth from the consummate wisdom and manifold bounties of your Lord and the all-encompassing mercy of the Beloved of your hearts.

26

He is God.

1   O thou beloved scion of him that hath been immersed in the ocean of divine forgiveness! A long time hath passed since I last wrote. This hath been due to the

numerous occupations that deny me a single free moment and that are, moreover, compounded by woes and trials. Among other things, in these days 'Abdu'l-Bahá hath once again been confined to prison in 'Akká by reason of the great mischief stirred up by the people of malice and the lengthy letters teeming with disruptive charges against him that they have dispatched to Constantinople, as well as other devices to which they have resorted and which it is not advisable to mention here. Those who are prey to pride and vainglory had hoped that this calamity would only afflict 'Abdu'l-Bahá, oblivious that by their actions they shall cast themselves into the pit of everlasting disappointment and misery, and that they too shall suffer imprisonment.

This episode is similar in every respect to that of Yaḥyá. 2 He too imagined that his sedition would cause harm and injury to the Blessed Beauty. It was for this reason that he sent Siyyid Muḥammad to Constantinople and resorted to innumerable ploys and devices, until at last he exposed Bahá'u'lláh to great danger. But as soon as the fire of rebellion blazed, it immediately consumed Yaḥyá's own home. He was exiled from Adrianople, even before the Blessed Beauty. "They lost both this world and the world to come; and this, verily, is but evident loss."[38]

'Abdu'l-Bahá exulteth with boundless joy at these trials and tribulations, inasmuch as after the Ascension of the Abhá Beauty the loved ones of God find their happiness in tumult and trouble, and their felicity in ceaseless 3 afflictions. That is, the depths of the pit are for them the apex of heaven, and the straw mat of hardship is a kingly throne. Confinement in bonds and fetters is their highest aspiration, and captivity in stocks and chains their true freedom and a source of incomparable joy and delight.

4   It is evident that the joy of these homeless wanderers is not found in music or song or play, but rather consisteth in long-suffering in the face of hardships, patience in the midst of calamities, detachment from all created things, exaltation of the Word of God, and diffusion of the holy fragrances. Verily, this is grace abounding, and verily, this is manifest bounty. Upon thee be greetings and praise. Dispatch thou copies of this letter to far and near.

27

He is the All-Glorious.

1   O ye loving friends of 'Abdu'l-Bahá! It is early morn-ing and I have returned to Haifa from the Shrine of the Báb—may my soul be offered up for His dust. I spent last night within the precincts of His exalted Sanctuary, and through the blessings of that sacred Shrine I was filled with boundless fervour and joy throughout the night. The sweet savours of holiness wafting from His resplendent Sepulchre so perfumed my soul and caused my heart to quiver that my thoughts turned towards you spiritual friends, and I

began to write this letter. Despite countless concerns and manifold vicissitudes, I have set all aside and called to mind the countenance and character of the beloved of my heart and soul. Consider how great is my affection for you!

Your city was honoured for a long time by the foot-steps of the Blessed Beauty.[39] Tablets were revealed continually therein, and those who attained His presence hearkened to His blessed Words. Among them was a well-known Persian who associated with Him. This person was secretly an intimate and close companion of the Ambassador, who sought his counsel on various matters. The Blessed Beauty was forbearing towards this man and turned a blind eye to his behaviour. And he, imagining Bahá'u'lláh to be unaware of his hidden motives, professed devotion to Him.

Finally, one day the Blessed Beauty addressed him thus: "I have a message for his Excellency the Ambassador. Convey it to him, saying: 'Thou hast done thine utmost to shed Our blood, and hast imagined thyself capable of uprooting this sacred Tree. But how far, how very far is this from the truth! This blessed Tree is immovable and its roots are firmly fixed; no axe can sever them, even should all the kings of the earth arise with all their might to do so. Though I stand alone and forsaken, yet I single-handedly withstand the world and all the peoples and governments thereof. Erelong, these dark clouds shall be dispelled and the Sun of Truth shall shine resplendent in the plenitude of its glory. Yea, indeed ye can take My life, and that would be the greatest gift of God, for it is through blood that this blessed Tree doth grow and flourish. Ye had imagined that if the Exalted One—may the souls of all on earth be offered up for Him—were martyred, this Divine Edifice would be subverted. Therefore did ye make His sacred breast the target of a thousand bullets. But ye then saw the Cause of God become more manifest and its light stream out even brighter, such that it hath now reached Constantinople!

4 "'Do ye then imagine that if ye were to cut the throat of Bahá and spill the blood of this people, the flame of the Lord's burning Fire would be extinguished? God forbid! Nay, rather, the Word of God would be further exalted, and the Sun of Truth would be revealed in still greater splendour. Soon the day shall come when ye shall all be doomed to disappointment and loss. Carry out whatsoever is in your power. O Áqá Mírzá! All this injustice, this hostility, animosity, and cruel tyranny is, in our estimation, nothing more than the buzzing of a gnat. We attach no importance, therefore, to thy rancour or cruelty. "And they who act unjustly shall soon know what lot awaiteth them."[40] We paid no attention whatsoever to thee or to the Ottoman government when We arrived in Constantinople. This fact alone should awaken thee to the truth that Our trust is placed in the power of God and His dominion, and in naught else. All kings are but His subjects, and all such as thee are immersed in a sea of loss and perdition. In time ye shall behold it. Persia

shall fall into ruin, and her government and people shall be afflicted with dire hardship. We, however, have shed illumination upon that land and have desired eternal glory for her people. Though at this time Persia standeth obscure amongst the nations, the day shall come when this mighty Cause will have made her people most honoured and esteemed by the whole world.'" In brief, the Blessed Beauty continued to speak in such severe terms. That person left and never returned.

Now, praise be to God, a fragrant breeze hath wafted ⁵ over Constantinople which shall perfume that land with musk. The friends must conduct themselves with the utmost constancy, steadfastness, and wisdom, and remain perfectly assured. My fervent hope is that each one of them may become even as a brilliant light, and that the Divine Teachings, which are the source of illumination for humanity and the cause of the peace and tranquillity of the world, may be diffused with the utmost wisdom. This sea is turbulent and its tides are mounting high. I implore Him tearfully at eventide and at dawn, supplicating His unfailing aid and assistance for the beloved of the Lord. The Glory of Glories rest upon you.

28

He is God.

1 O ye dear friends of 'Abdu'l-Bahá! After his visit to the Sacred Threshold, and the Centre round which circle in adoration the Concourse on high, Jináb-i-Fárúqí came to stay with 'Abdu'l-Bahá and was for a few days his companion. He was in a state of supplication to the Abhá Kingdom, and of ardent devotion to the Concourse on high. He recalled the friends of God one by one, and with an aching heart and tearful eyes begged that a special letter be written to each of them.

2 But 'Abdu'l-Bahá hath not a moment's calm nor an instant's rest; he hath no free time whatsoever. Were he to divide his time into the minutest of fractions and dedicate each of them to communicating and corresponding with a different group, he would still be unequal to the task. Praised be God! The believers throughout the East and the West are surging like the waves of the sea, requiring at least ten contingents of secretaries to reply to their letters in an adequate manner. It is, therefore, not possible, alas, to fully satisfy the request of each and every pilgrim. As a result, I am abashed and filled with shame and embarrassment, wondering in what tongue to voice my excuse to Jináb-i-Fárúqí. I have found no recourse but to write one detailed letter collectively to all the friends, so that several copies may be made thereof and presented to each of

the believers. No remedy is there now but to make do.[41] There is a well-known saying: "The part testifieth to the whole, and the drop telleth of the pool."

And now, in these days when the Lord's burning Fire ₃ hath set the world ablaze, when the light of His effulgent glory hath illumined the East and the West, when the pervasive influence of His Word hath dazzled every mind and the Cause of God hath gained such ascendancy as to leave no peril or reason to fear, the claimants have seized the chance to enter the arena.[42] Those who until now had remained silent in their corner of oblivion, those frightened bats that had, from the pulpit-tops of Iṣfahán and Ṭihrán, recanted their faith in the Báb—may my life be offered up for Him—have now rushed forward to lay claim to primacy. They have stealthily convinced a few heedless ones of their claims and scattered the seeds of doubt. They are now hounding this and that person in the utmost secrecy, either to deflect him from the straight path or to harm him in some other way.

Friends and strangers alike know that, during the days ₄ of peril, the leader of these people roamed throughout the land in the guise of a dervish and went about, bowl in hand, asking for "alms for the sake of God". After the episode of Ṣádiq and Náṣiri'd-Dín Sẖáh,[43] he abandoned the believers in the district of Núr to the threat of the sword and chains, and fled at once into hiding in Mázindarán and Gílán. He tied a cord round his head, put on the cloak of a dervish, and, adopting the name "Darvísẖ-'Alí", roamed the plains and mountains until such time as the Blessed Beauty was banished to Iraq. He then followed Bahá'u'lláh to Baghdad, taking shelter under His protection but still in hiding and in abject fear of everyone.

5 Subsequently, the Blessed Beauty left for Kurdistan. The early believers of Iraq and Persia are all well aware that, during the absence of the Most Great Name, Mírzá Yaḥyá travelled in disguise in the regions of Súqu'sh-Shuyúkh and Basra, under the name of Ḥájí 'Alí. He carried some Arab slippers and thus became known as Ḥájí 'Alí the shoe-seller. Later he proceeded to Najaf, bought some silk, and was referred to as the silk merchant. He even dressed in Arab garb and abandoned his Persian name. During the two-year absence of the Blessed Beauty, the Cause of God was left with neither name nor fame.

6 In the aftermath of the martyrdom of the Báb, and during the absence of the Desired One, that unchaste one engaged in such a disgraceful act as would have been repulsive even to the notorious Ghayúr of Baghdad.[44] That is, after the martyrdom of the Báb, he wedded the wife of the Exalted One, the Mother of the Faithful, marriage to whom had, according to His explicit statement, been forbidden to all.[45] And as if that dishonour were not enough, when he found her not to his liking, he presented that honourable lady—the sister of Mullá Rajab-'Alí and the wife of the Báb—to Siyyid Muḥammad-i-Iṣfahání. This was the extent of his exertions, his claim to might, power, and fame: to busy himself, by day and by night,

in multiplying the number of his wives. He even summoned his own wife's sister, Ruqíyyih <u>Kh</u>ánum, from Mázindarán, and married her too, thus being "married to two sisters at the same time".[46] He also wed the sister of Mírzá Naṣru'lláh-i-Tafri<u>sh</u>í. The mother of Mírzá Aḥmad, too, was one of his lawful wives, and he further entered into matrimony with the daughter of an Arab, thus transgressing the limits set by the clear text of the Bayán. These are his numerous marriages in Baghdad alone and do not include the ones in Ṭihrán and Mázindarán. Should ye investigate the matter, the truth of this verse would be made clear and evident: "He was calamity itself, that huntsman who passed through our grove."[47] We shall not expatiate further on this matter. The point is simply that that "paragon of chastity"[48] carried out such acts as are contrary to the explicit Text revealed by the Merciful Lord, and spent his days and nights in these vain pursuits.

Dear God! In what way did he assist the Faith during this time? How did he serve the Cause of the Most Exalted One? Is there anyone who could claim to have been taught the Faith by him? Was he able, during his forty years in Cyprus, to guide a single soul? Nay, he was incapable of educating even his own children. Could greater incapacity be conceived than this? "They call upon that beside God which can neither hurt them nor profit them. Surely, bad the lord, and, surely, bad the vassal!"[49] 7

When the Blessed Beauty returned from Kurdistan, 8

only a small band of believers had remained in Persia, and those in Iraq had grown dispirited and had sunk into apathy. Not a murmur was heard anywhere, nor a single sound. Any believers who were still present were in the depths of apprehension, fear, and despair. Upon His arrival in Baghdad, however, the Most Great Name flung open the doors and issued a universal summons. The call of God was raised and the fame of His Cause noised abroad. Day and night, the leaders and the learned from amongst all peoples attained His holy presence. The flow of questions and answers was constant, and one and all testified to the sufficiency of His replies.

9   As a result, fear and dread caused Náṣiri'd-Dín Sháh to grow impatient and agitated. He resorted to every measure, and wrote a letter in his own hand to Sulṭán 'Abdu'l-'Azíz requesting the banishment of the Blessed Beauty beyond Baghdad. He claimed that Persia was in danger, that the government was greatly alarmed, and that harm would ultimately befall both governments. Thereupon, 'Abdu'l-'Azíz issued his decree for the departure of the Blessed Beauty. Yet, although subject to banishment and exile, Bahá'u'lláh nevertheless moved with the utmost dominion to the garden of Najíb Páshá, where for twelve days the Cause of God was exalted to such an extent that the Governor, Námiq Páshá; all the high-ranking officers of the army and the province; the country's religious dignitaries; and the nation's notables came by day and by night to attain His presence. All this, notwithstanding the

fact that He was, to outward seeming, an exile! Yet the pervading influence of the Cause of God, the sublimity of His Word, and the diffusion of the divine fragrances were such that those few days were passed in intense joy and delight, and the Riḍván Festival was inaugurated. Bahá'u'lláh then departed with the utmost sovereignty, and to this all the people of Iraq bear witness and testify.

But that "paragon of chastity", dressed in the garb 10 of a dervish and accompanied by a certain Arab named Ẓáhir, at one time contemplated journeying to India, and at another considered travelling to the regions of Egypt. He finally sent word, saying, "I am afraid to stay here after your departure, so I will hasten to Mosul and await your arrival there." At that time, it was rumoured that the Blessed Beauty and the company of His followers were to be delivered up to the Persian authorities in Karkúk, a city between Mosul and Baghdad, near the Persian border. For this reason, he said that he would join us in Mosul, because he assumed that whatever was to transpire would take place before our arrival in that city.

When we reached Mosul, a tent was pitched on the 11 bank of the Tigris, where the notables of the city, officials, and others flocked in groups to His blessed presence. One night the above-mentioned Arab, Ẓáhir, arrived, saying that the individual in question was lodged at an inn out-side the city and wished to meet with someone. My uncle Mírzá Músá went in the middle of the night to meet him. Mírzá Yaḥyá enquired about his own family and was told that they were among the companions and had their own tent, and that he could join them, should he so wish. He said, "I do not at all consider it advisable for me to do so, but there is a caravan which will be leaving at the same time as yours, and I will be among that group." Thus did he reach Díyár-Bakr, with a black cord round his head and an alms-bowl in his hand, consorting only with the Arabs and Turks in the caravan. At Díyár-Bakr he sent word, saying, "I will spend the nights with my family and will return to my caravan in the morning." This too was carried out. Since Ḥájí Siyyid Muḥammad knew him from before, he recognized him on sight and visited him, saying that he was a Persian dervish and an acquaintance of his. But as the other friends had not seen Mírzá Yaḥyá before, they did not at first recognize him.

12 So it was, until a disagreement arose between him and Siyyid Muḥammad. At that juncture, the "paragon of chastity" came into the presence of the believers who are still with us, and complained about Siyyid Muḥammad. When Siyyid Muḥammad entered Bahá'u'lláh's presence, he said, "I disagree with him on a particular question. He saith that a Mirror always sheddeth light, and I say that it is possible for a Mirror to become veiled; it shineth as long as it is turned towards the Sun, but the moment it turneth away it becometh dark."[50] The Blessed Beauty rebuked the Siyyid, saying, "Why dost thou dispute and argue and cause strife in the company of the friends?"

13 Subsequently Bahá'u'lláh's convoy arrived, in the utmost

dominion, at the Seat of the Royal Throne,[51] and He comported Himself with all-sufficing glory. The Most Great Name did not meet with any of the ministers or representatives, nor did He pay them the least attention.

29

He is God.

O thou who art steadfast in the Covenant! Thy letter of 12 Dhi'l-Qa'dih 1337[52] was received, but the earlier one hath not arrived. Thou hast written that, as a result of the attacks of the enemies, thou and thy father were forced to leave your home.

It hath ever been thus: Abraham departed from His native land, but His departure became the cause of joy. Moses was sent far from His homeland, but that exile led Him to behold the Fire upon Sinai. Joseph was made a homeless wanderer in Egypt, but He rose from the depths of the pit to reach the apex of heaven. Jesus was forced to leave the Holy Land for Egypt, but this separation became the cause of blessings. Muḥammad fled from Mecca to Medina, but His flight resulted in victory. The Báb was likewise banished from Shíráz to the banks of the river Araxes, but auspicious indeed were the results of His banishment! The Blessed Beauty—may my soul be offered up for His loved ones—was exiled from

Persia to Iraq, thence to Constantinople, and later to the Land of Mystery,[53] before being transferred to the Most Great Prison. All these successive banishments became the cause of the illumination of the East and the West. Now ye too have suffered your share of banishment and exile; rest assured that great results shall ensue. Praise be to God that Munír, like the resplendent morn, hath become radiant and illumined with the splendours of teaching the Cause!

3   As to thy question: Know thou that in all created things sweetness and bitterness are accidental attributes. That which, through its elemental composition, appealeth to the sense of taste is conceived as sweet by the palate, and that which runneth counter to it tasteth bitter. These are both accidental attributes; they are not due to any difference in essence.

4   Man, however, hath a twofold station: one luminous, the other dark; one pertaining to the realm of the Divine, the other to the world of nature; one inclined towards heavenly virtues, the other towards satanic qualities. For man standeth on the demarcation line between light and darkness. In the circle of existence, he is situated at the lowest point, which marks at once the end of the arc of descent and the beginning of the arc of ascent. For this reason, he is free to move in either direction: towards light or darkness, towards ignorance or guidance—depending on the one that prevaileth. Should the rational faculty prevail, man would shine radiantly and occupy a lofty station

in the realms on high. And should the self and the lower nature prevail, the result would be darkness and he would fall into the nethermost fire. For in man the powers of the heavenly Kingdom and the forces of his animal nature are at war until one or the other doth triumph. The Glory of Glories rest upon thee.

30

He is the All-Glorious.

O tender twig of the blessed Tree! Thy numerous letters have been received, and their spiritual meanings were honey-sweet upon the palate of the soul. All praise be unto the All-Glorious Lord, Who, through the fragrant breezes wafting from His Abhá Kingdom, hath revived and refreshed that verdant branch, that tender twig, and hath graciously aided thee to strive in the path of His good-pleasure.

O thou who art attracted to the divine fragrances! The resplendent Beauty of the Almighty, the radiant Sun of the Realm of Glory, hath arisen above the horizon of the world, shedding the lights of sanctity upon both East and West. Though possessed of immortal glory and holiness, that hallowed Being endured manifold trials and tribulations and accepted every affliction and calamity. He tasted deadly poison from every cup and drank bitter venom from every chalice. He was bound in chains and fetters and held in iron shackles. In the dungeon, His companions were criminals, and His associates transgressors and evildoers. He was subjected to vengeance and torment; He was banished from His native land and exiled to Iraq, and thence to Adrianople. He was beset by denial and disdain and suffered at the hand of every oppressor. He was made a target for the darts of hatred and malice and was assaulted by the shafts of hostility and injustice. He was consigned to the Most Great Prison and condemned to its oppressive confines. At all times, He was under the threat of sword and spear, a captive and a prisoner.

3 His one and only purpose in accepting such trials and tribulations for His blessed Self was to instruct the lovers in the ways of love and teach the longing souls the art of servitude, to guide the yearning ones to the right path and summon the friends with words such as these: "If ye lay claim to faith and certitude, if ye are enthralled by the Beauty of the Merciful and have surrendered your hearts to His delightful splendour, if ye are enraptured by His Countenance and ensnared by His flowing locks, drink deep of the cup of woe as if it were the chalice of immortality, and welcome the sting of death as the elixir of life. Abandon all rest and comfort, and turn away from the defilement of this world. Consider the desert thorn as the softest silk, and regard the scorching fire as a flowering rose-garden. Drink the brine of bitter torment as if it were a fresh and thirst-quenching draught, regard the

point of the arrow as a wellspring of life-giving waters, and yearn for the sword and shaft as ye would the nectar of peace and security. Be ye exhilarated with the wine of tribulation, and take pleasure and delight in the sweetness of affliction."

Given these trials and tribulations of the Blessed 4 Beauty—may my life be a ransom for the earth ennobled by the footsteps of His loved ones—can we yearn for any greater gift than affliction in His path? Can we seek any balm other than a wound suffered for His sake, or any remedy except pain itself? Can we wish for any refuge save moments of fear, or any haven other than occasions of abasement? Can we hasten to any field but the arena of sacrifice, or desire any solace for our souls save the blade of tyranny? Nay, by Him Whose might extendeth over all things!

O my Lord! Graciously assist me to remain faithful and 5 steadfast in Thy Cause amidst all peoples. Aid me to drain the cup of woe, to be immersed beneath an ocean of trials and tribulations, to drink deep from the chalice of affliction, and to be invigorated by the gentle breaths of faithfulness in Thy path, O Thou in Whose grasp are the kingdoms of earth and heaven! Thou, verily, art the All-Bountiful, the Most Exalted.

Read thou this letter in the gatherings of the friends. 6

31

He is God.

1 O ye two handmaidens of Bahá! The Ancient Beauty, the Most Great Name—may my life, my soul, and mine inmost being be offered up for His sacred dust— was burdened with anguish at every breath. At one time, He was a captive to unyielding cruelty, and at another, a target to the darts of woe. At one time, He was a wanderer on the plain of Bada<u>sh</u>t, and at another He suffered the tribulations of Níyálá. At one point, He was bound with chains and shackles, and afflicted by grievous torment in Ámul; at another He had for associates His most despicable and cruel enemies. By day He was assailed by sorrow and grief in Karbilá; by night He lay within the embrace of afflictions in the camp of adversity. One day, He was conducted in chains, with bared head and bare feet, all the way from <u>Sh</u>imírán to Ṭihrán. There He remained in confinement for four months, weighed down with fetters and irons and threatened at every breath by blades and arrows. At another time, He was exiled to Iraq, and at yet another He roamed the wilderness of Kurdistan, where the birds of the air and the beasts of the field were His only companions. For many a long year, He was beset from all sides by the onslaught of His foes in Baghdad, and was encompassed by the fiercest woes and troubles. Every day brought a fresh adversity, and every night season

an arduous calamity. Not for a moment did He rest; not for a second did He find repose. He was then exiled to the Great City[54] and was pierced by the arrows of gross calumny. Men of high rank and stature arose, one and all, to denigrate Him, whilst the leaders of nations were intent upon His demise. Thereupon they banished Him to the Land of Mystery, where they submerged Him in dire adversities and woeful tribulations.

At this time, the one whom He had, with loving-kindness, nurtured in His own bosom ever since his earliest years, the one upon whom He had showered at every moment His tender care, rose up against Him with passionate hatred and assailed Him like a horde of calamities. Mírzá Yaḥyá even attempted to shed the sacred blood of the Ancient Beauty, and like a venomous viper he pierced the blessed body of Bahá'u'lláh. Mírzá Yaḥyá then began to moan and lament, and raised the cry of the oppressed, claiming to be an innocent victim and alleging that he had been most grievously wronged. He wailed and groaned, sighed and moaned. And like the envious brothers, he cast the Joseph of the Egypt of Existence into the depths of a darksome pit. He then raised a plaintive cry, sobbed and wept, and made manifest the verse "And they came at nightfall to their father weeping."[55] And then he began to keep company with the estranged, and became a confidant of the enemies. He accused the Peerless Beauty of having committed mischief and sedition, and he circulated leaflets of falsified Text amongst the malicious. All this, in order to extinguish the candle of the Company on high, consign the celestial Teachings to oblivion, turn the Morn of divine Oneness into night, and cause the Day-Star of Truth to set, the verses of guidance to be annulled, and the banquet table of the Eternal Covenant to be brought to naught.

3   Thus, confinement in the Most Great Prison came to pass, and inexorable adversity ensued. The Wronged One of the worlds fell prey to the people of iniquity, and suffered fresh trials and new afflictions at every hour. Every door was shut and every way was barred. The darts of tyranny descended upon Him in ceaseless showers from every land, and the swords of iniquity were drawn against His luminous and ethereal Being by the hosts of the earth. In brief, at each breath He was beset by the cruelty of a capricious foe, and at every moment He was afflicted and oppressed by a fresh sorrow, until at last His Countenance was veiled from the horizon of the world and shone forth from the firmament of the Placeless. And now, from the horizon of that Kingdom, He beholdeth how the hosts of this nether world have launched their assault upon His lonely servant, and how the rising tide of tribulation hath engulfed His forsaken bondslave. I swear by His exalted Essence that the eyes of the Concourse on high weep with a great weeping, and the lamentations of the dwellers of the Abhá Kingdom have stirred the realities of earth and heaven. For the trials that have afflicted this servant are innumerable, even as thou knowest and dost witness.

Let not your hearts be saddened by this calamity, nor 4
grieved over this affliction that hath come to pass. Set your
hearts upon the mercy and the loving-kindness of the Abhá
Beauty—may my life, my soul, and mine inmost being be
offered up for His loved ones. Rejoice in His glad-tidings,
and take delight in His manifold favours. The ocean of His
favours is limitless, and the sweet savours of His bounty
spread far and wide. The eye of His tender mercy watch-
eth over all, and His overflowing grace is vouchsafed unto
all, especially unto you who are the remnants of the King
of Martyrs and the victims of oppression in the path of
the Almighty! The gaze of His particular loving-kindness
is directed towards you, and the radiance of His special
bounty is cast upon you. Wherefore, render ye thanks unto
the Beloved for having been favoured with such bestowals
and made the recipients of such mercy. The glory of God
rest upon you, O kindred of the King of Martyrs.

32

O beloved friends of 'Abdu'l-Bahá! No sooner had 1
the Hand of divine power raised the tabernacle of
everlasting glory—the tabernacle of the oneness of humanity—in the midmost heart of the world, than He opened
wide the portals of supreme mercy before us all, addressed
us in hallowed accents in the Hidden Words, honoured us
with the title of "O My servants", associated us with His

own Self, and freed us from distress and fear. He spread wide the banquet table of bounty and issued a universal invitation. He prepared for us all manner of heavenly food and bestowed upon us divine favours and heavenly gifts. He delivered us from every heavy load and relieved us from every grievous burden. He enjoined upon us only laws, ordinances, and teachings that bestow life to the soul and cause it to draw nigh unto the Best-Beloved.

2   His laws all grant liberation rather than restriction; they confer freedom rather than limitation; they impart joy and radiance rather than constraint. The laws and ordinances of all former religions included the waging of holy war, resorting to bows and arrows, swords and spears, chains and shackles, and the threatening and beheading of every hostile oppressor. But in this wondrous Dispensation, the Blessed Beauty hath delivered the friends from this heavy burden. He abrogated contention and conflict, and even rejected undue insistence. He exhorted us instead to "consort with the followers of all religions in a spirit of friendliness and fellowship". He ordained that we be loving friends and well-wishers of all peoples and religions, and enjoined upon us to demonstrate the highest virtues in our dealings with the kindreds of the earth. He even regarded enemies as friends, and considered strangers as comrades and intimate companions. What a heavy burden was all that enmity and rancour, all that recourse to sword and spear! Conversely, what joy, what gladness is imparted by loving-kindness!

Now, in gratitude for these infinite bestowals, it behov- 3
eth us to arise to carry out the counsels and admonitions
of the Blessed Beauty, and to act in accordance with His
teachings and ordinances. We must strive with heart and
soul to drink a brimful cup of this heavenly wine, that our
words, our deeds, and our conduct may be those of the
righteous. We must show forth love and kindliness, and
demonstrate, through our faith and sincerity, that we are
all servants of His Threshold, and true and steadfast keep-
ers at His door. We must prove ourselves Bahá'ís in reality,
and not merely in words.

'Abdu'l-Bahá yearneth to join the friends in servitude 4
to the Threshold of Bahá, but he is abashed and doth sigh,
lament, and repeat this verse by day and by night:

Before the Friend how can I ever lift my face,
Abashed that I did naught to befit His grace?[56]

The Glory of Glories rest upon you.

33

He is God.

O thou scion of a cherished friend! Thy letter was 1
received in Alexandria. It was long since there had
been any news, and so it brought gladness and joy.

2   For forty-three years, 'Abdu'l-Bahá was a prisoner in the city of 'Akká, during which time he conducted affairs in such manner that even strangers acknowledged them to be, under all circumstances, in accord with the good-pleasure of the peerless Lord. His love, affection, care, and consideration for every soul were such that all the peoples and kindreds marvelled at it; each and all showed the utmost respect and reverence.

3   At first, the decree of the iniquitous sovereign was most harsh, placing Bahá'u'lláh in such strict captivity that even I would be denied access to His holy Presence. Nay more, the Ancient Beauty was to be confined alone and forsaken, and to remain under vigilant watch day and night. However, the conduct of 'Abdu'l-Bahá was such that the pavilion of the Blessed Beauty was finally pitched with utmost dominion and majesty upon Mount Carmel, and His blessed Being came to reside outside the citadel of 'Akká, living with the utmost might and honour in the only mansion of that region, utterly detached from all others.

4   Indeed, the Governor of 'Akká pursued me unrelent-ingly for five years, begging permission to attain His holy Presence, but the Blessed Beauty would not grant him leave to do so. One day, this servant set out to attain the presence of Bahá'u'lláh, and started walking from 'Akká towards the Mansion. All the officials and even the Governor himself accompanied me on foot. The Governor, Abázih Páshá, happened to be a stout and corpulent man.

Sweat began to pour off him as he walked, and it was in such a state that we arrived at the Mansion. The Blessed Beauty—may my life be offered up for His loved ones—did not even deign to enquire after them.

There was a time when another governor arose against 5 us in hostility, and took sides with the government commission. This governor induced someone to send secretly a document containing strange allegations against us to the royal court, which then returned the document and called for an inquiry. The Governor and the delegation subsequently wrote a harshly worded report, evincing great enmity and hatred towards us. However, this servant dismissed the Governor and the delegation. Such the degree of our influence, as is known to friend and stranger alike.

Now our so-called friends have brought matters to 6 such a pass that we must be forbearing even with a low-ranking officer. They have carried their flattery to such extremes that it hath become necessary to waste all our time, spending our days and nights countering their slanders. These friends are continuously seeking every means in their power to hurl grievous calumnies at 'Abdu'l-Bahá, that perchance he may be banished from the city of 'Akká and they may find a vast arena in which to spur on their chargers.

I have, however, of mine own accord undertaken a 7 journey to this land[57] and have left the arena to them, so that it may become evident that, even in my absence, they are not and never shall be capable of making a move, however inconsiderable, except to flatter this or that person. Even should the nightingale forsake the rose-garden, the raven and the crow would still not acquire any charm.

8   In brief, we are at present engaged in serving the Sacred Threshold in this country, and we fain would hope that this journey may yield fruit, and that we may advance and exert ourselves in the field of servitude. Pray ye fervently, and with tears supplicate His Kingdom of sanctity, that in thraldom to the Threshold of Bahá this servant may be, however slightly, delivered from shame. Perchance, God willing, he may be graciously aided to attain a dewdrop of the ocean of servitude, for thus far he hath achieved naught but regret. If it please God, perchance aid and confirmation from the Abhá Kingdom may be vouchsafed unto him in the days to come, and this cherished hope may be fulfilled, if only to a small degree.

9   Praise be to God that thou, the son of one who is well favoured at the Threshold of the Lord, art attracted to the Kingdom of Abhá. Should thy business bring thee on a journey to these regions, perhaps we may meet undisturbed in this vast land.

10   Thou didst write regarding the gatherings of the friends held every Sunday for the purpose of reading the holy verses and reciting prayers. This brought immense gladness and joy to my heart.

11   Convey my Abhá greetings to the humble and well-favoured handmaid of God, thy mother, and to thy

84

brothers. Convey also my heartfelt greetings to Jináb-i-'Abdu'l-Mihdí—upon him rest the glory of God, the All-Glorious. Give him my warmest love, and tell him on my behalf: "The clamour and tumult raised by that furtive man is of less significance than the buzzing of a fly. Thou art well aware of the root cause of the shame and abasement that he hath chosen for himself. Those who went before him in bygone centuries serve as a lesson for him.[58] Yet, alas, alas! How the veils of tyranny have covered their eyes! Erelong will they find themselves condemned to utter loss. Verily this is the truth, and naught is there beside the truth but grievous error."

This person saw how the pre-eminent leaders of the 12 past fell into ruin as a result of their deviation, and to what a state of utter loss they were reduced. Despite this, he was not chastened; he continueth to attempt these futile deeds. After the advent of the Spirit,[59] there appeared individuals such as Arius who had a million followers. These people later disappeared without a trace, and no sign of them remaineth. The glory of God rest upon thee.

34

He is God.

¹ O ye twin shining stars! Praise be to God, for your faces are resplendent with the light of guidance, and your dispositions are pleasing and favoured at the Divine Threshold.

² Ye have asked for permission to come on a visit. The Holy Land is indeed the niche from which the Light shineth, the lamp in which the Sinaic Flame is burning. In this sacred land the Blessed Beauty unveiled His countenance, and from it He addressed Tablets and proclamations unto all the kings and rulers of the earth. To attain the honour of pilgrimage is the cherished desire of His lovers, and to circle round His Shrine the highest hope of those who yearn after Him. Yet, service to His Threshold rendered in your land is also among the supreme aspirations of those who are nigh unto Him. Nevertheless, the choice is yours. The Glory of Glories rest upon thee.

35

He is the All-Glorious.

O ye true friends! The letters ye wrote, the pages ye penned, and the names ye mentioned were all received in the Holy Land; they have all been attentively perused, and their most pleasing contents have been noted.

Praise be to God that through the grace and favour of the Ancient Beauty—may my life be offered up for His loved ones—such servants have been gathered beneath the standard of the Covenant as have perfumed the world through the gentle breezes wafting from the gardens of their hearts, and flooded the realm of splendours with the light shining from their faces. They are the manifestations of the manifold bounties of the ever-living Lord and the exponents of the signs and tokens of the Great Announcement. They are the dawning-places of the stars of guidance and the daysprings of the mysteries of loving-kindness, the sweet savours of the rose-gardens of Divine Unity and the fragrances of the meads of Oneness, the immovable mountains of the Covenant and Testament and the well-springs of the soft-flowing waters of joy and certitude, the fruitful trees of the paradise of faith and the birds of holiness soaring above the meadows of understanding, the shining lamps in the assemblage of divine mysteries and the embodiments of purity in the gathering of the righteous. They are graciously aided by the hosts of the Abhá

Kingdom and favoured with the assistance of the angels of the celestial Concourse.

3   O ye loved ones of the Abhá Beauty! O ye friends of the Almighty Lord! Unloose your tongues in thanksgiving for this supreme bestowal, and render praise unto the peerless Lord that ye were singled out for this grace and favour, and numbered amongst those who have attained the heights of servitude. Gird up the loins of endeavour, and step into the circle of the angels of the paradise of Oneness. Thus may ye, on the shores of the Most Great Ocean, net the fish that thirst for the seas of divine knowledge and, in the fields of unity, catch the gazelles that seek the meads of reality, so that through the unfailing aid and bounty of the Lord, ye may gather together all nations beneath the shade of the Word of Oneness. Thus may the fragrances of God spread through the East and the West, and the magnetic forces of the All-Merciful stir the world of being into motion. Thus may the mysteries of this holy Cycle be made manifest, the signs of the Dispensation of the Most Great Name be revealed, the garden of the world be rendered fertile, and the orchard of creation bear luscious fruits. Thus may the candle of Divine Unity be kindled, contingent limitations be consumed away by a single flame of the Lord's burning Fire, the lights of guidance shine, and the darkness of ignorance and blindness be utterly obliterated.

4   When Christ winged His flight unto the limitless realms, He left behind eleven disciples. As they arose, with

a seeing eye and a hearing ear, with an eloquent tongue and an unshakeable resolve, to magnify the Word of God, they so flourished that each became like unto the tree whose "root is firmly fixed, and whose branches reach unto heaven, yielding its fruit in all seasons".[60] Simon Cephas,[61] who was the shining moon amongst those stars of guidance, was to outward seeming no more than a fisherman on the Sea of Galilee. And yet, because he arose with fixed resolve and the utmost vigour to spread the signs of God and gather together the righteous, the light of his servitude shone with such brilliance above the horizon of existence that the very sun and moon were left bewildered, and circled, moth-like, around that resplendent candle.

Now, upon His ascension, the Ancient Beauty—may [5] my life be offered up for His Most Great Name—left behind some fifty thousand believers upon this swiftly passing world. He educated them, one and all, through the sweet scents of holiness, opened the doors of manifold grace before their faces, nurtured them in the bosom of His loving-kindness, and taught them the lessons of the spirit in the school of insight. Would it not be regrettable if we were to sit dispirited or remain lost and bewildered, if we were to prefer the path of comfort and repose, seeking freedom from all cares? This is not faithfulness! This is not sincerity! This is not the path of guidance!

Erelong our days shall draw to a close, and the birds of [6] the meadows shall carol the anthem of departure. Erelong the lamp of health shall be quenched, the darkness of

89

death shall prevail, and the resplendent morn of the life to come shall dawn. Let us then strive with earnest endeavour to arrive at the heavenly Kingdom with radiant faces and, in the Realm of Glory, be admitted into the circle of those who have remained fast and firm. Consider what a fire of guidance eleven souls kindled on the summits of the world when they endured all manner of woes and trials and arose with all their hearts! Now, were we to arise as we ought, armed with the assured confirmations of the Abhá Kingdom, what splendours would be made manifest and what results would ensue! I swear by the Beauty of the All-Praised, by His upraised standard, and by His sheltering shade, that such a conflagration would blaze up in the heart of the world as would melt the very rocks and clods of earth.

7   O friends, make ye a mighty effort! O loved ones, arise and bestir yourselves! Occupy yourselves not with the tales and accounts of those who waver in the Covenant, for these are but confused dreams and idle and childish talk. Speak of them that are steadfast, and tread the path of them that stand unwaveringly firm.

The duty of long years of love obey,
And tell the tale of blissful days gone by.[62]

36

He is the Most Glorious.

O thou verdant, fresh, and radiant leaf! Were we to weep and moan for a hundred thousand years at this Supreme Affliction,[63] to sigh and lament, to rend our garments in sorrow, to shed tears and heap dust upon our heads, and to pine away with grief, this pain would never be stilled, this wound never healed, this fire never quenched. It behoveth us, therefore, to see ourselves, at every breath, as standing ready to depart to the next world, and to arise to carry out that which is conducive to eternal life and would cause us to ascend unto the Kingdom and to attain the court of His Presence. The glory of God rest upon thee.

37

He is God.

O thou who hast fixed thy gaze upon the Kingdom of Glory! The splendour of the Beauty of the world illumined the whole earth, conferring heavenly grace upon all created things. The Beloved of the world shone forth, captivating His lovers with His charm. And now, though that Sun hath set, He still shineth resplendent from the unseen Kingdom, continuing to bestow eternal grace upon all regions. Those that are possessed of insight perceive the world to be illumined with the splendours of the Sun of Truth. But those whose inner eye is dimmed are deprived of beholding the light: They pronounce day to be night and proclaim morn to be eve.

2   Say: O hapless one! That Sun shall never set, nor shall that Day-Star of the Realm of Glory ever wane. The setting of the sun is only in relation to the dwellers of the earth, for how can there be any daybreak or nightfall in the sun itself? It remaineth ever shining in its meridian splendour, ever glowing and luminous, at the sublime apex of bounty. The Glory of Glories rest upon thee.

38

He is the All-Glorious.

1   Those loved ones of God who have turned from the Mosaic gulf towards the ocean of the Almighty Lord and the billowing waters of His Ancient Beauty have at all times been remembered in the court of His manifold bounties and in the presence of the Lord of Hosts. Now that the Day-Star of the heaven of holiness hath ascended unto the Most Exalted Kingdom and dawned above the horizon of the all-glorious Concourse, every firm and

constant believer is mentioned in that Realm of sanctity in the august presence of the Beloved.

Despair not over this grievous calamity, this dire afflic- 2 tion. For although the Ancient Beauty is now hidden from the horizon of the world, His light shineth forth from the heaven of eternity, in the Most Great Kingdom. Was the eternal radiance that shone forth from the horizon of Moses in bygone days extinguished after He ascended to the realms above? Nay, by the righteousness of the Lord! It rose and shone even more intensely, and the bright flame of the remembrance of God blazed even higher. Now once again, ye shall behold how the resplendent lights of Divine Unity will erelong envelop the kingdom of existence, and the ensigns of His words will be raised upon the loftiest heights of the realities of all beings.

Esther was a woman; when she was favoured with pure 3 intent and turned her gaze unto the Lord, what services she was enabled to render! Now behold the tomb of this woman of noble birth, and consider the myriads of mighty kings who ruled over Persia, Transoxania, and other countries in the world. Neither name nor fame nor trace doth remain of any of those kings; all have faded into utter nothingness and have been utterly abased. Yet, as this woman who was the pride of all men drew a breath in the path of the All-Merciful, the influence of her actions still endureth, and her name is, to this day, mentioned amongst the loved ones of God. Take ye good heed, O people of insight!

39

He is God.

O Thou Whose exalted Threshold is my haven and my refuge, Whose hallowed Sanctuary is my shelter and my abode! I entreat Thee, with a heart aglow with the fire of Thy love, and with eyes streaming with tears in my longing to attain Thy presence, in my yearning to gain admittance into the Kingdom of Thy glory, and in my desire to taste the sweetness of faithfulness to Thee, to graciously aid this servant through the breaths of Thy holiness and the delight of communion with Thee. Render victorious, O my God, by the hosts of Thine all-glorious Kingdom and the waves of the seas of Thine all-encompassing bounty, this servant of Thine, who is enraptured by the company of Thine angels on high and enkindled with the fire of Thy love amidst Thy servants. He is engaged in serving Thy Cause amongst the peoples of the world, and in magnifying Thy name before the ministers and rulers. He is occupied in diffusing Thy sweet savours in gatherings held in remembrance of Thee, and hath hoisted Thy banner amidst the masses. He hath turned his face towards the Court of Thy grandeur, and is illumined with the light of unwavering constancy in Thy Covenant and Testament. He is striving to enable all to remain steadfast in that which Thou hast enjoined upon the entire company of Thy chosen ones, which Thou hast foreordained for them that are dear to Thee, and with which Thou hast sealed Thine ultimate decree.

O Lord! Assist him through Thine invisible hosts, and 2 strengthen him with the might of Thy holy angels. Make him a brilliant star, a radiant orb, a manifest light, a breeze from the meadows of Thy glory, a fragrance from the flowers of the plain of Thy mercy, a ray of light from Thy divine Kingdom, a bright beam from the sun of the heaven of Thy Oneness, and a standard rippling on the summits of Thy great majesty and singleness. O Lord! Strengthen his loins by Thy triumphant might, and sustain him amidst the people through Thy glorious sovereignty. Grant that all hearts may be attracted to him, all minds astounded in his presence, and all ears made attentive to his utterance; that, moreover, all eyes may turn their gaze towards his cheerful countenance and all hearts marvel at the brightness of his face. Thou art, verily, the Most Powerful, the Most Exalted, the All-Glorious, the Ever-Forgiving, the Most Compassionate, the All-Loving.

In these days, although this lowly one hath no time 3 or respite whatsoever for correspondence, yet the sweet savours of the love of the beloved of God have so enraptured my heart that, when writing, the reins of volition slip from my grasp and the words flow unrestrained. In particular, whenever my thoughts turn towards thee, whose heart is attracted to God, the act of writing bringeth me joy and happiness, and setting pen to paper is conducive to delight. Hardship turneth into gladness of the heart, and toil is transmuted into blessing for the soul.

4   This is the day when we all should gather beneath the shade of the Word of Oneness. Let us burn even as bright candles in every gathering; let us be aflame with the fire of love. Now that the Beauty of the All-Praised hath ascended, and the Day-Star of the Kingdom hath set, whither can we direct our affections, and what comfort can we expect? How are we to find repose, and in what hope can our hearts rejoice? O the pity! A myriad times the pity, if for a single moment we should look for ease or comfort. Alas! A thousand times alas, if we should seek any peace and tranquillity except in trials, tribulations, and suffering sustained in His path.

5   That sanctified Being spent His days in chains and fetters, and lived to the end of His life under the threat of the sword. Not a moment's rest did He find; not a tranquil breath did He draw. Not for a single night did He repose on a bed of comfort, nor lay His head upon a pillow of ease. Every bird hath a nest, and every creature dwelleth in its abode, while the Blessed Beauty was consumed by the fire of cruelty lit by His enemies. The people of the world are asleep upon the couch of ease, while the Most Great Name found not a moment's rest, nor drew a single breath in peace. By what standard of fairness or fidelity can we seek repose or pursue comfort and rest?

6   Praise be to God that thou art engaged day and night

in serving the Cause of God, and art earnestly striving to diffuse His fragrances and to propagate the splendours of the light of His knowledge. By thy very life! This is a bounty from amongst the bestowals of the Lord, one that no other bounty in the world of being can ever rival. Erelong its splendours shall shine forth and its musk-scented breaths be shed abroad; the gentle breezes of its meadows shall waft and the soft-flowing waters of its fountains flow. Thereupon, thou shalt see those who taunt and mock yielding thanks, and those who sigh and complain rendering praise. Thou shalt behold the envious becoming remorseful, and the slandering women cutting their hands, exclaiming, "Great God! No mortal is this! This is no other than a noble angel."[64] "Verily, there is a prosperous issue to the God-fearing."[65]

In brief, after His ascension, He Who is the Self- 7 Subsisting was faithful to His promises. He vouchsafed a remedy to heal the hearts, and caused the gentle breezes of joy to waft. He aided His loved ones with the hosts of the unseen, and confirmed them with the power of the Kingdom. He assisted the friends throughout the earth, and succoured His loved ones in every land. The radiance of His glory spread throughout the East, and His influence was made manifest in the West. His enemies were brought low in all regions, and His foes were everywhere left friendless and forlorn. Each mighty one was rendered weak, and every haughty stirrer of mischief was abased, with none to help them.

8   Consider how, through the operation of invisible means, the foolish ones of the earth arose to foment discord and strife, made the government of Persia exasperated, engaged in rebellion, and raised a tumult. It became thereby clear that they were the root of all mischief and the source of all malice. Thus were the promoters of peace distinguished from the seditious, and the ensuing events exposed their hidden secrets. Thus was it made plain that they were wolves in the guise of shepherds and thieves garbed as watchmen, an oppressive darkness in the world and a formidable obstacle to the well-being and prosperity of all.[66]

9   In like manner, a group of foes gathered in the Great City and sought through every ruse, plot, and stratagem to bring ruin to the Cause of God, to disperse the gathering of His loved ones, and to cause a breach amongst His people.[67] I swear by the Ancient Beauty! When that company of foes joined hands with the shameless Jamálu'd-Dín,[68] they kindled such a fire of sedition in the Great City that it was feared its flames might reach the lofty abode of Him round Whom circle all that dwell on earth, and that the resulting damage might threaten the very foundations of the Cause of God. Then did the Hand of Omnipotence emerge from His unseen Kingdom and disperse that company in such wise that it was reduced to a handful of scattered dust and condemned to eternal perdition.

Therefore, in thanksgiving for His divine confirma- 10
tions, let us strive by day and by night to exalt His Word,
to be consumed by the fire of His love, and to raise our
voices in His remembrance and praise. Given such tender
mercies, such bestowals, such aid and assistance, how can
we remain still? How can we sit silent? O how pitiful it
would be, were we to tarry, to hesitate, or to fail to offer
up our souls! How pitiful, were we to set our hearts on
ephemeral attachments rather than quaff of this mystic
wine! Woe unto us should we remain occupied with
our selfish desires, busy ourselves with our own earthly
concerns, and follow the promptings of such passions as
deprive us of these bounties and deny us a portion of
these bright effulgences. By my life! This, verily, would be
naught but manifest loss.

40

He is the All-Glorious.

O God, my God! Thou hearest my sighs and bitter 1
wailing, my cry and the voice of my lamentation
in the depths of these darksome nights. Thou seest my
abasement and lowliness, my patience and resignation,
my poverty and urgent need, my anguish, my distress, my
grief, and my sorrows throughout my days.

2   I render Thee thanks, O Lord, for this tribulation, which I deem amongst the greatest of Thy bounties and gifts, for it is endured in the path of Thy love—a love whose flames blaze within my very heart and soul. This is my wish and my hope, O my God. This is a soothing balm for my anguish, O my Best-Beloved; a cooling draught to these parched lips, O my Healer; the remover of my sorrows, O Thou Who art my Friend.

3   I raise my suppliant hands in prayer to Thee, beseeching Thee at every morn and eventide, seeking shelter at Thy sublime and most exalted Threshold, pleading for the intercession of the Primal Point, Him Who is the Word of Thy oneness, Him Whose breast was riddled in Thy path by the myriad bullets fired by the enemies; and I adjure Thee by that hallowed Beauty Whom Thou didst make a companion of Thy divine countenance when the Dayspring of Thy resplendent Sun shone forth upon the Supreme Horizon, to ordain for this servant of Thine the chalice of selflessness from the hands of bounty, to lift the veil so he may ascend towards Thy sublime Threshold within Thine all-glorious Kingdom. Deliver me, then, from the onslaught of the people of malice, from the darts of slander and rancour raining down upon me, from the successive assaults of the arrows of animosity, and from the spears of calumny hurled in continuous succession by the leaders of men. Thou art the God of bounty, the Compassionate, the All-Merciful.

4   O thou friend of 'Abdu'l-Bahá! Although the Sun

of Truth hath set on the horizon of this nether world, yet grace and bounty are His, for He shineth forth with extraordinary brilliance from the hidden realm of souls, above the horizon of the unseen Kingdom.

After His ascension, all the governments and peoples 5 of the world expected that His luminous Orb would set and His sheltering shade would be withdrawn. They waited for His upraised standard to be hauled down and the light shining from His brow to fade away and be no more. All grace and bounty are His; for instead, the lamp of His Cause glowed luminous, and the morning light of His loving providence shone resplendent. The Sinai of His oneness was exalted, and the Summit of His single-ness was raised to even loftier heights. The standards of His sovereignty were unfurled, and the signs of His might were made clear and evident to every discerning soul. The drumbeat of His Divinity reverberated, moreover, throughout the world, and the bell of His Lordship pealed out the triumphal summons of "Yá Bahá'u'l-Abhá!" from East and West. At one time, it kindled its flame in Amer-ica; at another it shed its radiance upon Africa, and upon the Turk and the Tajik. At one time, it raised its call among the Slav; at another it set Cumania ablaze. Its fame hath now been noised abroad throughout the world, and all the peoples and kindreds of the earth are in search of it.

And yet, some thoughtless individuals loudly clamour 6 that the darkest of nights hath arrived and the deepest gloom hath enveloped all, that the Cause of God hath been abolished and His Law annulled, that another hath laid claim to a new revelation, raised the cry of "Verily, I am God", and exalted himself above the Ancient Beauty.[69] Their purpose is to use these false and foolish statements to conceal their own violation and to shroud the tabernacle of the Covenant of the ever-living Lord under the frail webs they have woven. Though immersed in the depths of idle fancies, yet with their lips they profess the one true faith of God. Though violating the Covenant, yet they utter the name of the Day-Star of the world. Though they linger in the darksome night of doubt, yet they cry out: "Where is the light that shineth on every side from the unseen realm of the All-Glorious?"

7 Certain pure souls, such as Mírzá Abu'l-Faḍl—upon him rest the glory of God, the All-Glorious—are engaged day and night in demonstrating the truth of this blessed Cause through conclusive proofs and clear testimonies, recounting the facts and removing the veils, propagating the Faith of God and diffusing the divine fragrances. Meanwhile, other individuals, like unto birds of night, strive to sow the seeds of doubt and are detested and estranged. Behold how great is the difference in their ways! Our purpose is to fill the whole world with the fragrance of musk, while others seek to torment the senses of all peoples and nations with the foul odour of dissension.

8 At times, they even accuse this servant of claiming Divinity and assert this allegation to be the basis of their hostility, whereas 'Abdu'l-Bahá would never barter

servitude at the Sacred Threshold for the sovereignty of both worlds; indeed, the dust of that Sacred Threshold is his refulgent diadem. But the Slanderer, in a document that is still extant, written in his own hand and bearing his own seal, hath proclaimed himself to be the Sun of Truth and laid claim to a revelation greater than that of the Blessed Beauty. The following are his very words: "By the righteousness of the Lord! The Greater Day-Star of God hath appeared, before whom every other sun is punier than the puniest of things." And he goeth further still to say, "These verses were revealed to me while I was still a child." The Blessed Beauty rejected this claim of his, and it was at that time that He revealed a Tablet stating: "Should he for a moment pass out from under the shadow of the Cause ...", and so forth.[70]

Indeed, in my own writings there doth exist a passage stating that the Sun of Truth rose from the zodiac sign of Aries and is now shining resplendent in the sign of Leo. This servant is still present! As thou hast said, they must address their questions to me rather than give interpretations according to their own vain imaginings and personal motives. In making such a statement, I had in mind no one else except the Báb and Bahá'u'lláh, the character of whose Revelations it had been my purpose to elucidate. The Revelation of the Báb may be likened to the sun, its station corresponding to the first sign of the Zodiac—the sign Aries—which the sun entereth at the Vernal Equinox. The station of Bahá'u'lláh's Revelation, on the other hand, is represented by the sign Leo, the sun's mid-summer and highest station. By this is meant that this holy Dispensation is illumined with the light of the Sun of Truth shining from its most exalted station, and in the plenitude of its resplendency, its heat and glory.

10 As to the words "may all eyes be illumined", these are from the revered martyr Varqá—may my life be offered up for him. What thou hast written is correct.

11 And furthermore, regarding the statement "He who summoneth mankind in My Name, he verily is of Me", these are the blessed words of the Abhá Beauty—may my life be offered up for His loved ones; the statement is not mine. How grievously hath he erred who reported such a thing, who spread it abroad, and who repeated it. "Feeble indeed are the seeker and the sought!"[71]

12 God grant that through the celestial might of the Kingdom and the power of the Covenant, and through heavenly inspiration, thou mayest withstand the insinuations of the sowers of doubt, for their whisperings utterly quench the flame of the Lord's burning Fire in the hearts. Kindle thou a flame, and set ablaze the fire of the love of God! The glory of God rest upon thee.

41

He is the All-Glorious.

Glorified art Thou, O God! The least of the signs of Thy Kingdom is, under all conditions, sanctified above all description and praise, and every single reality in Thy dominion is exalted beyond the highest tributes of the people of the world; for the very essence of remembrance is wholly removed from the One remembered, and the inner reality of all praise remaineth veiled from the One praised. The signs of Thy dominion, in their very essence, are immeasurably exalted above the reckoning of the exponents of praise, and are sanctified beyond the grasp of them that are endued with understanding. The most eminent of sages have acknowledged their failure in this regard, confessing that their minds can fathom only that which is within the measure of human capacity and commensurate with the power of the birds of mortal thought when soaring in the heights of knowledge.

O my God! Given such clear and evident powerlessness, such plain and manifest poverty in recognizing the least of the signs of Thy dominion in the world of creation, how then can I unloose my tongue to make mention of Thine attributes and to proclaim Thy virtues? How can I speak forth Thy praise and celebrate Thy glory in Thy presence? How can I extol the evidences of being and the realities of existence that are found in the world of allusions and the realm of creation?

3   I have no recourse but to proclaim: "Hallowed and sanctified art Thou! Immeasurably high, exalted, and glorified art Thou!" and to implore pardon for this sin and transgression of mine, which hath filled me with shame before Thy loved ones. For to proclaim Thy sanctity and holiness is naught but to venture to describe Thee and, as such, is an evident sin, a shameful and palpable error.

4   O Lord! I beseech Thee by the Hands of Thy Cause, the Daysprings of Thy remembrance and the Dawning-Places of Thy command, and by the coursing of the stars and the burning meteors that rain down upon them that deny Thy manifest Cause and stray from Thy straight Path, to assist Thy loved ones who are firm in Thy Covenant and Testament and steadfast in Thy love and remembrance. Help them attain unto every good Thou hast ordained in Thine all-glorious Kingdom. Thou art, in truth, the Powerful, the Mighty.

5   That which Jináb-i-Ismu'lláh had written was perused. He hath asked for provisions for the journey to the divine Kingdom, and spiritual sustenance for the world to come. As thou well knowest, in this day, such provisions consist in assisting weak souls to become firm and steadfast in the Covenant, diffusing the divine fragrances, protecting the stronghold of the Cause of God, and preserving the distinctive features of His religion. For in the Abhá Kingdom there is no greater gift than this, and among

the Concourse on high there is no offering more wondrous. It is therefore incumbent upon thee to strive to the
utmost, by day and by night, to carry out this important
task, so that no breach may be made in the unity of the
Word of God, and no divisions may arise in this mighty
Covenant and binding Testament. Alas for all whose feet
slip and whose hearts waver!

This servant's highest wish and greatest desire hath 6
ever been that we may all gather together beneath the
sheltering shadow of the Word of Oneness, wholly for-
getful of every vain imagining; that we may search for
none other than His Countenance, seek naught but His
abode, and commune only with Him. May we, in truth,
offer up our lives wholly for His sake, surrender ourselves
in His path, and strive to diffuse the sweet savours of the
Beloved far and wide.

For many years, Bahá'u'lláh nurtured these servants in 7
the bosom of His loving-kindness, and trained and educated us through His compassion and unfailing bounty.
Even as a tender and loving Teacher, He taught us—His
children—the requisites of courtesy. In the school of God
He instructed us, so that after the ascension of His radiant
Beauty we might arise to follow the example of the faithful, and strive to serve the Cause of God and glorify His
Word. He promised us His confirmations and assured us
of His assistance, saying, "Verily, We behold you from Our
realm of glory, and shall aid whosoever will arise for the
triumph of Our Cause with the hosts of the Concourse

on high and a company of Our favoured angels."[72]

8   Praise and thanksgiving be unto the incomparable Lord, Who hath fulfilled His promises and provided all that He had foretold. He hath levelled every rough and rutted road and made smooth every stony path. He hath opened the portals of victory and graced us with the sweet savours of the Holy Spirit. The hosts of His all-glorious Kingdom have rushed forth, and the countless legions of His Company on high have descended with their swords unsheathed. He hath scattered the armies of His foes and defeated the legions of His enemies. Moreover, He hath manifested the signs of His power in all parts of the world and revealed His mighty Cause in every land. The melodies of His holiness have resounded in Europe, and the signs and tokens of His Revelation have been made visible to the Bulgar and the Slav. In America, His lamp hath shed its light upon the darksome night and guided souls from near and far. The fame of His majesty hath been noised abroad throughout Persia, and His servants in Ṭihrán have come to be truly revered to a degree that is without compare in former times.

9   In the Great City, He hath, in these days, thwarted the proponents of the Evil One and exposed their mischief for all to see. He hath completely extinguished that fire and caused their tale to be erased from memory. Indeed, the gathering of the worst mischief-makers and fiercest calumniators of the Blessed Beauty in such a significant location, their incessant efforts by every means to bring

ruin to the Cause of God, and their resorting to all manner of whisperings and machinations posed a grave danger to the Cause and provoked grievous malice against the loved ones of God. They had firmly pledged, one and all, to throw this land into turmoil. Through the intermediary of Jamálu'd-Dín-i-Afghání, they had penetrated all the ministerial circles. By the aid of that person, they had even gained access to the private royal quarters. Yaḥyá's son-in-law became the personal secretary of Jamálu'd-Dín, and Shaykh Aḥmad was among the permanent members of his circle.[73] They uttered every possible calumny and seized upon every possible measure to subvert the Divine Edifice and harm these exiles.

Placing our whole trust in God, we held fast to the [10] cord of resignation, and with sanctified hearts we cleaved tenaciously to patience. At last, a hand emerged from the invisible Realm and tore asunder the veils of hypocrisy and deception of that slanderous band. Their mischief became apparent, their sedition clearly manifest. Their malicious scrolls were revealed, and they were afflicted with the retribution which such behaviour entaileth. They fell into the grip of justice and were sent to Persia. Take heed lest this matter be misunderstood by the common people.

The point is this, that after His ascension, the Ancient [11] Beauty graciously aided His blessed Cause a hundredfold and vouchsafed divine confirmations unto these helpless ones. All praise and glory, all reverence and honour belong unto such a Lord!

12   In brief, the greatest yearning of this servant is to fulfil this sublime aspiration, which is to serve the Cause of God. At no time have I ever cherished any desire of mine own, nor do I regard myself as having any existence before the signs of His Oneness. But I strive to safeguard the impregnable stronghold of His resplendent Cause. I am apprehensive of any corruption of the Text, of any false interpretation, of all discord and division, lest a thousand years from now such matters arise once more and cause a breach in the one true Faith of God. For such a condition would destroy the very foundation and utterly subvert the cornerstone of the Divine Edifice. We would, one and all, be left hopeless and deprived, outcast and condemned. The dispersion of the gathering of the friends and the scattering of the company of the believers would be so great that each one of them would be lost and forgotten in the wilderness of perdition. Naught would remain of the Temple of the Cause of God but an insignificant name in common histories. We must therefore bend all our energies towards keeping the stronghold of the Cause impregnable and its foundation inviolate.

13   Thou hast written concerning the holding of gatherings on the occasion of the Day of the Covenant. Nothing greater, more potent, or more momentous can be conceived than the Covenant of God and His Testament! No such thing hath ever occurred in the Dispensations of the past, that an explicit text should be so clearly revealed in such unmistakable language as in the Most Holy Book,

a quarter of a century prior to the ascension of its Author; that the Ancient Beauty should nurture and educate all His loved ones through this divine grace; that He should then enter, with His Sublime Pen, into this firmly established and mighty Covenant with them; and that He should mention this Covenant in all His Books and Tablets, encouraging and praising those who hold fast unto it and renouncing those who break it. By what means can the one who hath failed to cling to this firm cord and mighty bond be secured? All the chains and ties of the world would be incapable of binding him fast.

Should it be thy wish to provide the means of ensuring a firmer adherence to the Covenant, compile thou the words and verses that have been revealed in all the divine Tablets on the subject of the Covenant and the Testament, and, after reading the Book of the Covenant in that gathering, recite those verses, so that the station of the steadfast and the station of those who waver may be made clear. This matter is greater than all others. 14

42

He is the All-Glorious.

O thou who art aflame with the fire of the love of God! We hear that thou hast within thy being a blazing fire, and that thy soul, even as the winged moth, 1 is consumed by its flame. Within the lamp of thy heart is cradled a bright candle, and within the sanctuary of thy soul reigneth the Best-Beloved of every gathering. Gracious God! What a concealed mystery is this and what a wondrous reality: The once-cloistered Friend hath become renowned throughout the world, and the once-hidden Beloved hath been unveiled in every land!

2   That everlasting Beauty hath now ascended to the eternal Kingdom. That Day-Star of the realm of Divine Unity is now shrouded behind the clouds of the invisible world. Despite this, the spreading rays of His holiness shine resplendent from the wellspring of the hearts of those who embody His praise. And while the mighty Ocean is concealed in the dense clouds of the world, yet its majestic billows surge from the wellsprings of the realm of being and are visible upon the shores of existence. Thus, while hidden, He is manifest, and though wrapt in concealment, He standeth revealed above every horizon in the easts and the wests of the earth.

43

He is the All-Glorious.

1   Although the Sun of Truth may outwardly be veiled by the clouds of concealment, were one to look with a perceiving eye, listen with a hearing ear, and

ponder with an awakened heart, it would become evident that the splendours of the Most Great Light have grown stronger and the rays of the lamp of God waxed brighter, that the waves of His most mighty Ocean have surged higher and the outpourings of the heaven of His bounty have become more abundant and manifest. For, until now, the veil of the human temple hath been an impediment to beholding the Sun of Truth. But now, wholly sanctified from all earthly things, that resplendent Orb and Day-Star of the highest heaven shineth forth above the Supreme Horizon and beameth bright from the all-glorious Realm. This is His explicit text: "Verily, We behold you from Our realm of glory, and shall aid whosoever will arise for the triumph of Our Cause with the hosts of the Concourse on high and a company of Our favoured angels."[74]

Even as was clearly seen in the advent of past Manifes- 2 tations, only after Their ascension did the greatness of the Cause of God and the sovereignty of His Word become clear and evident. Consider, for instance, how during the Dispensation of the Spirit,[75] only a handful of seemingly humble souls were believers at the time of His ascension, and yet, when those feeble ones arose with supreme steadfastness, they were so assisted by divine confirmations and by the effusions of the Holy Spirit that they shone forth above the horizon of the world in such wise that the splendours of their imperishable light continue to illuminate both this nether realm and the realm beyond.

3   Hasten, then, O ye loved ones of God and His trust-
ees; hasten unto this most great favour! Rush forth, O ye
blessed and chosen ones among His creation, rush forth
unto this most exalted and august station!

44

He is the All-Glorious.

1   O thou who hast truly believed in the Ancient Beauty!
The King of eternal glory, the sovereign Lord, hath
been established upon the throne of grandeur and hath
shed abroad the splendour of all His names and attributes.
He, verily, hath seated Himself upon the Seat of Divinity and sent forth His universal summons. By "Seat" here
is meant the Cause of God and His religion, this glorious Dispensation and wondrous Age. And by "seated" is
meant His manifestation and appearance, His effulgence
and presence.

2   The brows of some were adorned with the brightness of this effulgent light, whilst others regarded this daybreak as powerful sorcery.[76] Gracious God! The dawn is
the same, the rising of the Sun is the same, and the Source
of all splendour is the same. Yet its effect is of two kinds:
"And we send down of the Qur'án that which is a healing
and a mercy to the faithful: But it shall only add to the
ruin of the wicked."[77] The glory of God rest upon thee.

45

Glorified art Thou, O Lord my God, my Master, and my Ruler! Thou seest me a victim of every tribulation, a target for every shaft, and exposed to every spear. Not a day passeth but that swords are drawn against me and afflictive darts are hurled successively at the breast of this servant of Thine who standeth poor and desolate amongst Thy creation. And yet, Thou seest how my heart is filled with joy through the breaths of Thy holiness, how my soul is enraptured by the signs of Thy oneness, how my eyes are solaced by beholding Thy lights, and how my spirit is exhilarated by the gentle breezes wafting from the meads of Thy loving-kindness! I pay no heed to these shafts and spears, nor am I perturbed by any other matter. Nay, rather, I cling to the hem of patience, wear the armour of fervent supplication, and quench the devouring flame ignited by the hands of the wicked doers, with the tears I shed by night and by day.

Assist me, by Thy strengthening grace, O my God, to serve Thee amongst the righteous. Graciously aid me to render service unto the pious, and grant that I may offer up my soul for the faithful among Thy servants. Permit me, by Thy manifold favours, O my Lord, to enjoy intimate communion with Thee, and have mercy upon me by Thy bountiful grace. Keep me safe within the stronghold of Thy care and Thy protection, and guard me from the onslaught of the enemies, whether it be openly

LIGHT OF THE WORLD

or privily inflicted. Cause me to speak forth Thy praise amidst Thy loved ones, and enable me to be a sign of mercy amongst the people. Help me, O Lord, to serve Thy loved ones throughout all regions. Thou art in truth the All-Bountiful, the Almighty, and verily Thou art the Compassionate, the All-Merciful!

3   O ye faithful friends of 'Abdu'l-Bahá! In this new springtime, the luminous Orb shone forth from the vernal point at the equator, shedding its splendour upon the world and bestowing, through its light and heat, a new grace and a potent spirit upon every region. Through that heat and light, energy and vitality were generated in the veins and sinews of the world, a new creation was called into being, and a fresh spirit was breathed into it. The weary frame of the world was endued with new life, and the dead body of existence was quickened and endowed with measureless blessings. A wondrous Dispensation dawned, a new creation was called into being, and the verse "I breathed of My spirit into him" was fulfilled.[78] The realm of being was adorned, and the universe was illumined by the dawning of that manifest Light. Signs of life and growth appeared in all created things, and great advances became visible in all beings.

4   Those who judge with fairness acknowledge that the nineteenth century was the era of light and the pride of all ages. The signs of progress became visible in every aspect of existence, in such wise that it became equal to a

hundred others. Indeed, the achievements of this one century were greater than those of the fifty that came before.
That is to say, were ye to gather the works, the inventions,
and the wonders of the previous five thousand years, they
would by no means compare with those in this heavenly
era and divine century. The enterprises and discoveries of
those fifty centuries, their sciences and inventions, their
achievements and wonders, cannot rival those of this
one century.

Behold, therefore, how the signs of the revelation of ₅
the Sun of Truth are present and manifest in all created
things! And yet, the ignorant and unheeding are sunk
in endless slumber. They remain utterly unaware of the
cause of this growth and development, and the source
of this boundless progress. They know not the Orb
whose dawning hath ushered in this divine springtime,
nor the clouds whose outpourings have brought forth
these boundless favours. They see the motion, but reflect
not upon its motive force. They acknowledge the fresh
beauty of the vernal season, but are utterly heedless of the
limitless effusions of grace in the divine springtime. They
see the rising dust, but cannot perceive the swift-riding
horseman. They gaze at the towering sails, but cannot
apprehend the onrushing winds that propel the ship.
They hearken unto the celestial Song, but remain oblivious to the Mystic Nightingale. They witness the surging
waves, but are blind to the boundless ocean. They feast

on fresh and luscious fruits, but remain ignorant of the Tree of mysteries. They see the lustre of the lamp, but are unaware of the dazzling light within it. In any case, it is our hope that the people may wake from their slumber, become inebriated by this choice wine, and, through its power, grow mindful.

6   O ye friends of God! Ye are truly intoxicated by the wine of fidelity; ye are indeed the victorious hosts of the Concourse on high. Ye have scattered far and wide and are assisted by the all-pervasive power of the Word of God. Ye are the means for the quickening of the peoples of the world and are leaders among the ranks of His true lovers. Ye are guides to the path of salvation, and your hearts are wedded to His clear tokens and signs.

7   O friends! Praise be to God that the banner of Divine Unity hath been hoisted in every land, and the melody of the Abhá Kingdom hath been raised on every side. The holy Seraph of the Concourse on high is raising the cry of "Yá Bahá'u'l-Abhá!" in the midmost heart of the world, and the power of the Word of God is breathing true life into the body of existence.

8   Wherefore, O ye faithful friends, it behoveth you all to join 'Abdu'l-Bahá in self-sacrifice and in service to the Cause of God and thraldom to His divine Threshold. If ye be aided to attain unto such a supreme bounty, the whole world shall erelong be made the recipient of the effulgent splendours of God, and the longed-for one-ness of humanity shall be revealed in the utmost beauty

and charm in the midmost heart of the world. This is the dearest wish of 'Abdu'l-Bahá! This is the greatest yearning of them that are faithful! The Glory of Glories rest upon you.

46

He is God.

O ye beloved of the Lord and handmaids of the All-Merciful! No sooner had the Sun of Truth shone forth from the heaven of sanctity than it shed upon the horizons of the world the light of unity of thought, unity of opinion, unity of belief, and unity of truth. And this, so that humankind might come together at one single point with respect to thoughts and beliefs; that quarrels, disputes, and conflicts might wholly disappear from amongst humankind; and that the same Light radiating from the Sun of Truth might illumine every heart. For the sake of this complete unity, this perfect harmony, His blessed Being endured every woe and all manner of trial and tribulation in such wise that eyes weep and hearts are for evermore consumed.

Praised be God that the beloved of the Lord in other countries in the East are one in belief, one in thought, and one in word, and are holding fast unto the same truth. But apparently, in some parts of America, differences of opinion have arisen amongst the believers. Such differences destroy the foundation of the Divine Edifice. For this reason, the Centre of the Covenant will now address this question in clear and explicit words, so that no differences whatsoever may remain, that the friends may be joined together and united, and that, by reason of this unity, the light of truth may illumine the world of humanity.

3　　The following is my explanation: The Exalted One, the Báb—may my life be offered up for Him—is the Promised One of the Qur'án, that is, the Mihdí, the promised Qá'im, Who was to appear after the Prophet Muḥammad. He is the bright Morn dawning from the horizon of guidance, and the Harbinger of the Abhá Beauty. The Blessed Beauty—may my life be offered up for His loved ones—is He Whom God shall make manifest, the One promised in all the Books and Tablets of the Báb. And 'Abdu'l-Bahá is the Centre of the Covenant of God, but the Branch is only an offshoot of the Tree. The Tree is the essence, the Tree is the foundation, and the Tree is the universal Reality.

4　　All the Scriptures have foretold the advent of two Manifestations, even as the Gospel doth refer to the coming of Elijah and the Messiah, by which is meant the Báb and Bahá'u'lláh. There is no third Manifestation.

5　　Whosoever may appear ere the lapse of one thousand years, even if he be endowed with utmost perfection, shall nevertheless be under the shadow of the Blessed Beauty and a servant unto Him. He will be the disciple of the Ancient Beauty, seek illumination from His light, and receive a share from the outpourings of His grace. Such a one may be likened unto a star or the moon, whereas the Blessed Beauty is even as the Sun itself. The moon acquireth its light from the sun. This is the sincere and heartfelt conviction of 'Abdu'l-Bahá. It is incumbent upon everyone to bear allegiance and cleave fast unto that which hath issued from the pen of the Covenant. This is the foundation of the Cause of God! This is the light of truth! This is the belief of 'Abdu'l-Bahá!

It is 'Abdu'l-Bahá's highest aspiration, therefore, to be 6 a true and faithful servant at the Threshold of the Blessed Beauty. Whosoever truly loveth me, whosoever is firm in the Covenant, must regard me as the servant of the Threshold of the Blessed Perfection. Nevertheless, it is unto the Centre of the Covenant that everyone must turn, for he is the Interpreter of the Book, and all the people of Bahá are under his shadow. Should anyone undertake, of his own accord, to interpret the Book of God in a manner contrary to the explicit text of the pen of the Covenant, it is to be rejected, for it would lead to disunity amongst the loved ones of God.

My purpose is to show that the Blessed Beauty hath 7 neither peer nor likeness. He is unique in His essence, and holy and sanctified in His attributes. I am under His shadow and the servant of His Threshold.

My hope is that following this explicit text which hath 8 proceeded from the pen of the Covenant, no differences whatsoever may remain, and that the American believers, even as the friends in Persia, may all become united in belief, thus rejoicing the heart of 'Abdu'l-Bahá and leading to the exaltation of the Cause of God in America. Publish this letter and circulate it throughout America. The Glory of Glories rest upon you!

9   Should a Persian come to those regions from the East—even, supposing the impossible, my son, or a daughter of 'Abdu'l-Bahá—without having a letter of permission in my handwriting and bearing my signature, it is forbidden to meet such a person or converse with him. For whosoever cometh without permission hath no aim save sedition and the violation of the Covenant.

47

He is God.

1   O thou twig of the Sacred Lote-Tree! The Dispensations of the past manifested either the splendour of the divine Beauty or the radiance of the divine Glory; either the dawning rays of "Verily Thou art of a noble nature" or the bright light of "God, verily, is wholly quit of the unbelievers";[79] either the effulgence of the manifest Sun or the gleam of the unsheathed sword. But in this great Cycle and blessed Age, despite the lack of an all-subduing power or earthly dominion, despite the absence of unsheathed swords or flashing spears, Glory and Beauty

have joined together and shone forth in a single luminous Countenance.

Though the Ancient Beauty—may my life be offered 2 up for His loved ones—was held alone and forsaken in the clutches of His enemies, though He was kept in chains and threatened by the sword, though He was banished to lands in Asia and Europe and finally exiled to the Most Great Prison, He ultimately rose in the utmost glory and beauty above the horizon of ancient might, manifest and radiant, resplendent and luminous, shedding light upon the world. All necks were laid low before Him, and all heads bowed down to Him; all faces turned humbly towards Him, and all voices were hushed in His presence.

48

He is God.

O ye homeless ones of 'Abdu'l-Bahá! Ye are homeless 1 and afflicted; ye are displaced and dispossessed of all, for your homes have been pillaged and your dwelling-places plundered. Ye have endured grievous trials, suffered dire iniquities, and been subjected, in truth, to the relent-less cruelty of the rebellious.

'Abdu'l-Bahá is also a captive in this Most Great Prison. 2 But I have found this prison to be a palace, and regard this bondage as true freedom. This cage is to me a heavenly rose garden, and this captivity an everlasting throne, for it hath befallen me in the path of God and for the sake of the love of the Abhá Beauty—may my life be offered up for His loved ones. How delightsome and pleasing it is! How sweet and precious! The trials and afflictions suffered by those friends have indeed been most grievous; yet, in truth, they are a flood of grace and a morn of hope to the hearts of those that are nigh to the Threshold of Singleness.

3   Consider what a blessing are calamities when endured in the path of God. The Prince of Martyrs[80]—may my life be offered up for Him—was plunged into the very depths of the ocean of tribulations, while the hostile Yazíd and the wicked Valíd seemingly prospered in the material world and relished its pleasures.[81] Later it became clear to all that those tribulations had been true blessings, while that prosperity was only divine chastisement and that pleasure naught but God's wrath and fury. The same holdeth true now. Although to outward seeming the divines and the unjust and foolish rulers are raising an uproar and flaunting themselves, erelong ye shall witness how, like the owls of the night, these people will creep into a desolate ruin, hasten to the tomb of eternal loss, and fall into the abyss of everlasting perdition. Even now, they wander distracted in the wilderness of disappointment, while the friends of God gleam brightly from the horizon of everlasting glory.

4   Were ye to consider carefully, ye would surely perceive

that adversity in the path of the one true God is a bounty, inasmuch as the Most Great Name, the Ancient Beauty—may my life be a sacrifice for His loved ones—did Himself endure a myriad afflictions. Now He hath granted that we, His lowly servants, may become His partners and associates in these trials and tribulations, each according to our capacity. Were one to judge with fairness, this suffering is worthy of gratitude, and these afflictions are naught but manifold bestowals. Upon you be greetings and praise.

49

He is the All-Glorious.

O thou whom the Lord hath aided to magnify His ¹ Word and to diffuse the sweet savours of the rose-garden of His holiness. Thou hast, for some time, been a companion of these enraptured souls and hast associated with these yearning ones in this Most Great Prison. Praise be to God, for thy brow hath been illumined and thy sight brightened by the dust of the sacred Shrine. Time and again, thou hast attained the honour of visiting the Exalted Threshold—that Spot round which circle the celestial Concourse, that Sanctuary of the denizens of the Abhá Kingdom—and hast detected the sweet scents of holiness.

2   Now, aided by heavenly power, divine strength, celestial attraction, and spiritual vigour; endowed with inner joy, a radiant countenance, an eloquent tongue, an outstanding utterance, and words of perfect praise; and confirmed by the outpouring flood of His Grace, return thou to the land of Ṭá', and thence to the land of Khá'.[82] Gather then together the believers in that land round the all-embracing Word, the luminous bounty, the manifest sign, and the glorious banner of the Book of God and His Faith, so that they may be revived and refreshed through the breaths of this supreme bestowal, and may be so set ablaze with the immortal flame kindled in the sacred Tree that each may become a kindled torch, a shining orb, and a brilliant star. The glory of God rest upon thee.

3   Convey my warmest loving greetings to the beloved of the Merciful, and tell them on behalf of this servant: "O ye who have quaffed from the Heavenly Cup, O ye who are attracted to the beauty of the All-Merciful! The Abhá Beloved and desire of the celestial Concourse—may I offer up my soul, my spirit, my life, my essence, and mine inmost being for His loved ones—throughout these long years endured all manner of trials and tribulations, woes and hardships, chains and fetters, and even this afflictive prison. All the while, He trained you beneath the shadow of the divine Teachings that ye might, on a day such as this, arise to proclaim the Faith of God and magnify His Word. Now is the time for you to forget all else but Him,

even as did the disciples of Christ. Now is the time for you to surge forth like a mighty ocean, that the sweet savours of God may perfume the East and the West."

50

He is God.

O thou who rejoicest in the glad-tidings of God! In every age and century, the Dayspring of the world is made manifest, shining with a particular splendour and revealed through a mighty sign. In the time of the Friend of God,[83] the horizon of existence was illumined with the lights of friendship. During the era of Him Who conversed with God,[84] the dawning-place of creation was brightened by the Light that glowed upon Sinai. In the days of the Spirit of God,[85] the realm of being was perfumed by the sweet savours of holiness. With the dawning of the Day-Star of Medina,[86] the horizon of the world was flooded with the light of love and grandeur. When the veil of concealment was rent asunder from the beauty of the Primal Point, the Morn of divine guidance was adorned with the resplendent rays of the most joyful tidings. And with this Most Great Revelation and the dawning of the Day-Star of the Ancient Beauty, the horizons of the world have been encompassed, blessed, and made evident and complete by all the divine bounties, effulgences, names, and attributes combined. For the Most Great Ocean possesseth and embraceth all the perfections that are to be found in every sea, gulf, river, spring, and stream.

2   This was written with a broken-nibbed pen. The pen hath been changed and the theme is now elaborated.

3   Consider the Writings of the Blessed Beauty on every matter, and the truth will become clear and evident. Examine the works of the Most Exalted Pen and compare them with all other Scriptures. Reflect upon the manifestation of His overpowering majesty, and ponder how in the Most Great Prison, singly and alone, with none to help or succour Him, He withstood all the peoples and governments of the world in the utmost sovereignty and glory.

4   For example, see how during the days of the Apostle of God—may the life of the worlds be offered up for Him—those who repudiated Him would say, as is clearly stated in the Qur'án: "And when they see Thee, they do but take Thee in mockery. 'What! Is this he whom God hath sent as an Apostle?'"[87] In this most mighty Revelation, however, the faithful as well as the froward, the rebellious, and the deniers all speak of the greatness of this Cause and the majesty of the Blessed Beauty—that is, even those that have not accepted and followed the fundamentals of His Faith. As thou hast witnessed, all the widely circulated publications of the world have testified to this. The humility and submissiveness shown by His enemies at all times, even within this afflictive prison, are

the greatest proof thereof, as are the signs of the influence of His dawning and transcendent Revelation, whose rays have been shed upon the whole world. Indeed, all historians have regarded this wondrous age, this new century, as the king of all ages and the sovereign of all centuries, and have regarded its achievements as transcending those of all previous ages. That is, shouldst thou compare the achievements of one hundred centuries to those of this single one, they could in no wise compare with it.

In brief, this Revelation is distinguished and excep- 5 tional in all respects. In gratitude for these bounties and bestowals, then, it behoveth us to forget all things in our yearning for the love of the Blessed Beauty and, with all our power and strength, centre our thoughts and words on teaching the Cause of God and diffusing the divine fragrances. In this day, this endeavour, that is, teaching the Cause of God, receiveth confirmation and is assured of victory by the aid of the hosts of the Abhá Kingdom.

I swear by the Ancient Beauty—may my life be offered 6 up for the dust ennobled by the footsteps of His loved ones! Were the weakest of all creatures to arise in this Day to fulfil this momentous task, that is, to diffuse the divine fragrances, it would become the mightiest of all created things. The drop would become like unto a sea, and the atom would attain the power of the sun. Although the hoopoe was a frail and feeble bird, yet the hosts of Solomon were its support. So it was that the Queen of Sheba, with all her legions, could not resist its powers and found no recourse but to surrender. Now, should any soul arise to diffuse the sweet savours of God, the hosts of the Abhá Kingdom will be his helpers and succourers, and the Almighty Lord his refuge and shelter.

51

He is the All-Glorious.

1 O thou spiritual physician! The body of humankind was afflicted with severe ills and chronic diseases, contagious maladies and prolonged fevers. Whereupon the ocean of divine favour surged, and the clouds of truth and bounty rained down upon the world of creation. The Sun of the firmament of Oneness shone forth, and vivifying breezes wafted from the meads of Singleness. The breath of the divine Messiah was diffused, the All-Knowing Physician appeared from behind the veil, and the skilled and true Healer emerged unconcealed. He prepared wholesome medicines from hidden substances, and created healing balms from concealed and treasured elements. He bestowed the panacea of unfailing efficacy, and conferred the sovereign remedy for every ill. He blended together spiritual elixirs, and created refreshing draughts made with heavenly pearls and rubies. And from the essence of Divine Unity and the quintessence of singleness, He taught and made known to us remedies that purify and tranquillize

and soothe. And all this, so that the feeble frame of the world might be freed from the burning thirst of error and ignorance, and this afflicted body might be delivered from the sore distress of heedlessness and impotence and attain unto a state of divine health and a well-being spiritual, complete, and absolute.

Yet ignorant and neglectful physicians devoid of learn- 2 ing have intervened and are preventing the divine and timely remedy from being administered. They prescribe instead that which causeth the aggravation of the disease and the worsening of the condition. Thou who hast discovered the storehouse of celestial remedies and the infallible divine medicines must strive, then, that haply the light of perfect health and unfailing tranquillity may shine forth even as the light of guidance from the Dayspring of healing, and that the obscuring gloom of ills may be dispelled and the deadly affliction of maladies eliminated.

52

He is God.

O thou servant of the Abhá Beauty! When the celestial 1 Lion rushed forth from the forest of the All-Merciful, He let out such a mighty roar that the sly foxes of ignorance and the cunning jackals, stained with the dye of deceit, fled the field.[88] They then began to plot and conspire, raised the dust of cruelty and malice, and abased themselves to the depths of degradation, and now bewail and lament in the remoteness of obscurity and extinction. Leave them, therefore, in their corner of oblivion. They are "those who forget God, and whom He hath therefore caused to forget their own selves".[89] Surely they are a people, evil, in grievous loss![90] Upon thee be greetings and praise.

53

He is God!

[1] O servant of the one true God! The Morn of divine guidance hath shed its radiance upon the East and lit up the Orient. It hath cast its beams upon the West and brightened the Occident. God be praised, for the renown and glory of the Abhá Beauty hath conquered the world, and the fame of the advent of the Most Great Name hath stirred up the whole earth. His call is now raised in every land, and His life-giving breezes blow from every region. Yet, regrettably, the unfaithful are striving to the utmost to extinguish His radiant Light, to still the wafting of His perfumed breeze, and to hinder the diffusion of His sweet fragrance. Alas, alas! Even if the dark clouds obscure the light of the sun for a while, they shall, in the end, be dispersed, and its effulgent rays shall shine forth once again. Upon thee be greetings and praise.

54

He is God.

O true believer in the verses of God! It is said that the greatest power in the world is the power of an all-compelling sovereignty and the might of an all-subduing government. However, the utmost that such might and power can achieve is to besiege men and conquer fortified strongholds. Such power and might is only made manifest by the aid of massed troops and conquering armies.

Yet, reflect thou on the power and ascendancy of the Greatest Name, on its might and dominion. Ponder how, though alone and forsaken, with none to help or succour Him, He, through the might and power of God and the sovereignty of the Kingdom, subdued the realm of being and conquered the citadels of the hearts of men. He prevailed over the whole world and established His authority over all existence. Single-handedly, He scattered the battalions of the earth; unaided, He defeated the unyielding hosts of darkness. In this day, the evidences of these victories exist in the invisible realm, but in the future they will appear in the visible plane as well. Then shall all witness the truth of the verse "Behold the confusion that hath befallen the tribes of the defeated!"[91]

Travel and explore the deserts—places such as the cities of Ṣáliḥ and Thamúd, the sand dunes of the tribe of Húd, the cities of Lot and of Sheba, and the settlements of the people of Rass and Midian,[92] and other lands. Behold how they have been, even as a defeated army, dispersed and scattered across these barren wastes.

4 My meaning is that although the Prophets of God and His chosen ones were, in every age and dispensation, alone and forsaken and subjected to relentless attacks by all the peoples and kindreds of the earth, yet their light shone bright and their stars gleamed resplendent, whereas the lamps of worldly power were extinguished, one and all.

5 He is God. O thou sanctified bough of the Tree of Holiness! Though that illustrious offshoot was severed from the garden of the contingent world, he hath been joined to the sacred Lote-Tree and hath grown fresh and verdant in the garden of the Placeless. He hath been nurtured from the wellspring of living waters and stirred by the breezes wafting from the bowers of the Abhá Kingdom. He hath entered the paradise of the Divine Presence, attained the court of the Almighty, and found his habitation in the bountiful realm of the All-Glorious.

6 And now, from the Concourse on high and the realm of effulgent glory, he beholdeth those that are left behind, and raiseth an inner summons for the heart and soul to hear, saying, "O my kindred, water ye all that I have sown, with the hands of faith and certitude. Nurture ye all that I have planted. Ye are the boughs and fruits of this bountiful tree; ye must reveal its true savour and fragrance and bring forth gem-like fruits. Be not dismayed by the winds

of tests, nor shaken by the tempests of trials. Let your roots grow deep in the soil of the Covenant and be nourished by the stream of the Testament of the Day-Star of the world. Hold ye fast unto the firm Cord, and seize the hem of the Covenant of the Lord of all worlds, that ye may become as fresh and graceful boughs that yield sweet fruits. This is my counsel and my admonishment unto you." The glory of God rest upon you.

55

He is the All-Glorious.

O thou who art inebriated by the heavenly cup! In the wilderness of Sinai in the Holy Land, in the hallowed precincts of the vale of Towa, upon the Mystic Mount from which the Light shone upon Moses, the Divine Lote-Tree was raised high, the Burning Bush was unveiled, and the Voice of the one true God was lifted up, raising a tumult in every land and resounding throughout the East and the West. Upon hearing this soul-stirring Voice, every attentive ear responded, "Here am I!" and cried out, from its inmost self, saying, "O our Lord! We have indeed heeded the Voice of Him that called us to the Faith of God—'Believe ye in your Lord'—and we have believed."[93] And every soul that was the embodiment of the verse "They are deaf, they are dumb, they are blind and shall return no more" responded, "Lo! This is naught but tales of the Ancients."[94]

2   Gracious God! Those who claimed to have heard the Voice of God calling from every least bush, rock, and clod of earth—even every blade of grass in the wilderness—rejected that Voice when its most wondrous accents rose from the Tree of Man with utmost eloquence and grace. This is a cause of astonishment, a source of pity. Thus shall the light of "He guideth whomsoever He pleaseth" be kindled and shine forth in the lamp of "He singleth out for His mercy whomsoever He willeth."[95] This, verily, is the truth.

3   Aid Thou Thy servant, O my Lord, who hath sought the light of Thy oneness from the Lamp of Thy guidance and hearkened to Thy most sweet Voice which hath been raised from Thy most glorious Kingdom. Assist him by the power of Thy triumphant might, and enlighten his heart by Thy Most Great Sign. Gladden his bosom through the sublime outpourings of Thy grace from Thine exalted Kingdom. Thou art, in truth, the Lord of this world and of the next.

56

He is God.

O ye beloved of God! O ye spiritual friends! The Lord 1
of the worlds hath said in the Qur'án: "A noble
pattern have ye in God's Apostle."[96] By this is meant that
the Prophet of God is the noble example to follow, and
that allegiance to that true Exemplar is conducive to salvation in both worlds.

The people of Muḥammad were enjoined to follow 2
His precepts in all matters and under all circumstances.
Those who saw this straight Path as the true Way followed
it and became even as kings in the realm of the righteous and the land of the chosen. And those who sought
their own ease and comfort deprived themselves of His
manifold bestowals and perished in the uttermost depths
of despair. Their days drew to a close, and their joys and
pleasures passed away. Their brilliant morn was turned
into darkness, and their clear chalice grew clouded and
was mixed with woe. Their radiant star paled and faded,
and their orb dimmed and set. But those holy souls who
walked in His ways beamed like guiding stars upon the
Supreme Horizon. They shone with incomparable light
from the dawning-place of all aspirations. They ascended
the throne of everlasting dominion and were established
upon the seat of heavenly delight. Their influence is still
manifest and their effulgence still resplendent. Their stars

shine bright, and their companions are the angelic hosts of the eternal realm. Lofty is their mansion, and unshakeable their foundation; their light illumineth the world, and their heat setteth the earth ablaze.

3   Now consider: If those souls who walked in the ways of that manifest Light attained such blessings and high rank, imagine what would happen were we to follow in the footsteps of the Abhá Beauty and the Báb—may my soul be offered up for them that have laid down their lives in Their path!

4   From the early dawn of the revelation of His beauty until the time of His most glorious martyrdom, the Exalted One passed every day and night in the most afflictive tribulations in the path of God. In the end, He made His breast the target of a thousand darts of woe and, with His breast torn to shreds, hastened to the Abhá Kingdom.

5   The Ancient Beauty, the Most Great Name, tasted the poison of every tribulation and quaffed from the brimming cup of every bitter affliction. He made His breast the target of every dart and readied His neck to every sword. He was cast into prison and bound by pitiless chains. He was beset by ferocious foes and attacked with stones hurled by the wicked. He was subjected to chains and fetters and confined to shackles and stocks. He was exiled from His homeland, banished to the lands of the Bulgars and the Serbs, and finally sore tried by grave affliction in the Most Great Prison. In this darksome pit, this prison of

tyranny, His blessed days came to an end and He winged His flight to His Kingdom.

And now, O faithful friends, O loved ones of that 6 luminous Beauty! Would it be meet and seemly for us to rest even for a moment? Would it be fitting for us to tarry or delay, to seek our own ease or comfort, thereby falling prey to idleness and tests, becoming preoccupied with our own fancies, and setting our affections on friend and stranger alike? Nay, by God! It behoveth us not to rest for a moment, whether by day or by night, nor to defile our pure hearts with the corruption of this world. We must spread a banquet of renunciation; hold a festival of love; lift up our voices and sing the blissful anthems of the Abhá Kingdom to the melody of the harp, the tambour, and the flute; and, hastening with joy and rapture to the field of martyrdom, surrender our lives and our all in His path.

O friends, show forth your fidelity! O my loved ones, 7 manifest your steadfastness and your constancy! O ye who invoke His Name, turn ye and hold fast unto Him! O ye who lift up your hearts and implore His aid, cling to Him and walk in His ways! It is incumbent upon every one of us to encourage each other, to exert our utmost endeavour to diffuse His divine fragrances and engage in exalting His Word. We must, at all times, be stirred by the breeze that bloweth from the rose-garden of His loving-kindness, and be perfumed with the fragrances of the mystic flowers of His grace. We must impart zeal and rapture to the hearts of the righteous and bring joy and ecstasy to the souls of the faithful.

8   Praise be to God that the hosts of His all-glorious Kingdom are rushing forth, the stars of His Most Sublime Horizon are shining bright, the banner of guidance is waving aloft, the showers of the clouds of bounty are raining down upon all, the Day-Star of the heaven of divine knowledge is shining resplendent, the joyful festival of the Kingdom is being held in the utmost delight, and the Morn of divine grace is casting abroad the rays of guidance. The anthem of the Abhá Kingdom can be heard from the celestial Concourse:

> O lifeless one, bereft of heart and soul,
> Come to life, come thou to life!
>
> O slumbering one, wrapt in mire and clay,
> Awake, do thou awake!
>
> O drunken one, so dazed and gone astray,
> Clear thy mind, clear thou thy mind!
>
> The world is filled with sweetest musk; the eyes
>   are brightened with His light; the heavens now
>   are set ablaze.
> From life and self be freed, be wholly freed!

Now is the time for sacrifice; here waft the breaths
of Paradise; secrets Divine are all made known.
Lead thou the lovers nigh, lead them nigh!

The sweetly singing mystic bird, upon a verdant
cypress bough, imparteth knowledge to the soul;
Commit His secrets to thy heart! Commit His
secrets to thy heart!

57

He is God.

O thou maidservant of God! Thy letter was received. [1]
Thou didst complain that your Assembly is sore perturbed. For every illness there is a remedy, and for every
affliction a relief. The swift remedy for this ill that hath
befallen the Assembly is to remember and reflect upon
the Covenant and Testament: Hath the Blessed Beauty
instituted this Covenant and Testament in order to exact
obedience from all, or to bring about disobedience? If
the latter is intended, then we have nothing to say; but
if obedience and compliance are the goal, then wavering
will lead to utter loss, and disobedience and waywardness
are grievous error.

Christ—may my soul be a sacrifice to Him—addressed [2]
but one statement to Peter, which He did not even

write down in His own hand, and it was this: "Thou art Peter, and upon this rock I will build my church."[97] Although this is one statement—not of such note—and although it was orally reported and not recorded by the Pen of Christ, yet all His Apostles submitted to it humbly and faithfully.

3   Now the Blessed Beauty hath—in His own hand, inscribed by the Pen of the Most High, and in explicit terms—emphatically enjoined allegiance and obedience upon all. So, one can either claim—God forbid—that the Blessed Beauty was ignorant, and that He erred in commanding all to obey the Centre of the Covenant and in explicitly appointing him as the sole Interpreter of the Book, or one must show forth obedience and allegiance. How strange! What answer will they give to the Blessed Beauty in the divine Kingdom? Such a reflection alone should suffice, were one to gaze with the eye of justice. But if there be no justice and words be guided by iniquity, then that is a different matter entirely.

4   In brief, these Covenant-breakers and their opposition are all even as the foam on the sea; it shall not endure, but shall pass away and vanish, while the sea itself, which is the cause of life, shall eternally endure. Consider the time after Christ. Regard how many souls arose to sow the seeds of mischief and sedition in His Cause but were eventually doomed to loss and disappointment, while the banner of Truth was raised aloft. So it is with

this violation of the Covenant. It is like a mirage and shall soon vanish into utter nothingness. Upon thee be greetings and praise.

Distribute numerous copies of this letter far and wide. 5

58

He is God.

O thou maidservant of God! Thy letter was received, 1 and its contents testified to thy firmness in the Covenant. Therefore, it is my hope that thou mayest be assisted under all conditions. In this day the most important of all things is to be firm and steadfast in the Covenant and the Testament, for Bahá'í unity can in no wise be preserved except through the Covenant. If it could be preserved by any other means, the Blessed Beauty would undoubtedly have decreed it.

In the Kitáb-i-Aqdas, unto which everyone must turn, 2 and in the Kitáb-i-'Ahd, which is the last Tablet revealed by the Blessed Beauty and recorded by the Supreme Pen, He addresseth everyone in clear and explicit terms, bidding first the Aghṣán, then the Afnán and His kindred, and finally all other believers, to turn unto the Centre of the Covenant. There is a verse revealed in the Kitáb-i-Aqdas exhorting all to turn, after His Ascension, to "Him Who

hath branched from this Ancient Root". In the Kitáb-i-
'Ahd, He testifieth in unmistakable terms that the object
of this verse is none other than the Centre of the Covenant. And in a specific Tablet, the authenticity of which
is admitted by everyone, He, in unequivocal language,
identifieth the Centre of Sedition by name, declaring that
should he pass out from under the shadow of the Cause
in the slightest degree, he would be cut off from the Holy
Tree.[98] How could anything be more explicit than this?
Now one must either say that the Blessed Beauty erred and
led the people astray, for He directed them to obey someone who ought not to have been obeyed, or else say that
the least deviation from the Covenant and the Testament
entaileth deprivation from the bounties of Him Who is
the Luminary of the world. Of these two alternatives, one
must be true; there is no third.

3   In sum, Bahá'í unity cannot be preserved save through
the Covenant of God. In this day, the dynamic power in
the body of the world is the Covenant; if the Covenant
be neglected, what other power can move it? The statement reportedly uttered by Christ to Peter, "Thou art
Peter, and upon this rock I will build my church", preserved Christian unity for a thousand years. After the lapse
of ten centuries, because of political reasons, dissension
arose. Now, if these words of Christ preserved the unity
of Christendom for a thousand years, it is clear what the
effect will be of the Kitáb-i-'Ahd, which was revealed by
the Supreme Pen! But certain restive souls—who were

at first firm in the Covenant and even wrote epistles, which are still extant, attesting to their firmness and their separation from the violators, and referring to the latter as outcasts from the Threshold of the Almighty—have now, because of personal interests, deviated from the Covenant and followed the people of malice. So it was with Judas Iscariot, who took part in shedding the blood of Christ for the sake of a few pieces of silver. Take heed, then, O ye who are endued with understanding!

If thou art firm and steadfast in the Covenant, let thy 4 ties with the Convention be strong and unassailable.[99] Turn away from, and stay clear of, any soul from whom thou dost detect the odour of deviation, that thou mayest be shielded and protected within the shelter of the Covenant, and mayest burn bright as a candle with the light of constancy.

I treat all people with kindliness and oppose no one. 5 I pray for all, that the glance of the eye of divine favour may be cast upon them. Verily it is the Blessed Beauty Who hath entered into this Covenant and Testament with all, not I. Let them answer to Him, for I raise no objections. My duty is to be kind to every soul; retribution is His and not mine. I show kindness unto all, and the purpose of every word that I write is to set forth the truth and to safeguard the Faith of God, so that Bahá'í unity may be preserved. Should some people attempt to undermine Bahá'í unity, the decision is theirs. Yet, what would they answer should the Blessed Beauty address them in the Abhá Realm in words such as these: "O Friends! Have I, through My Supreme Pen, and in explicit verses of the Kitáb-i-Aqdas, commanded you to show forth obedience or opposition? Have I not enjoined upon the Centre of Sedition himself to submit and to obey? How is it that ye have rejected My explicitly appointed Centre? I have commanded you to turn towards Him; wherefore have ye turned away and undermined Bahá'í unity?"

6   The friends must carefully examine all matters, and do as they deem fit. I have no obligation in this regard. Whatever voice is raised in America, there are always some ambitious and foolish souls who will gather around it for a while. Even in Green Acre, it was witnessed that a person from Malta invited people to starve themselves and received payment in return. Despite this, a number of people gathered around him. They were famished with hunger and lifeless as corpses, yet they rewarded him with money nevertheless!

7   Regarding thy dear brother who hath ascended from this mortal world to the eternal realm, grieve not and be not saddened. That drop hath hastened to the limitless Ocean; that homeless bird hath winged its flight unto the sheltering nest of the Concourse on high. Thou shalt find him in the assemblage of splendours in the Kingdom of mysteries.

8   As to thy dream in which thy brother appeared to thee finely dressed: Know that one's attire is one's adorning, which is the bestowal of the All-Merciful. As to the

parcel he had in his hand, this signifieth his benevolent deeds. The purpose of his intent gaze was to make thee understand his message, which is: "Behold the bounty with which I have been favoured! Praise be to God, for I am safe and well; I am attired in the garment of piety and carry the parcel of my deeds in my hand. I am alive, not dead—take heed! I am immortal, not ephemeral—take heed!" The Glory of Glories rest upon thee.

59

He is God.

O thou seeker after Truth! The statement of the Blessed Beauty which thou hast quoted doth supplement the verse "It is incumbent upon the Aghṣán, the Afnán and My Kindred to turn, one and all, their faces towards the Most Mighty Branch. Consider that which We have revealed in Our Most Holy Book: 'When the ocean of My presence hath ebbed and the Book of My Revelation is ended, turn your faces towards Him Whom God hath purposed, Who hath branched from this Ancient Root.' The object of this sacred verse is none other than the Most Mighty Branch ['Abdu'l-Bahá]. Thus have We graciously revealed unto you Our potent Will, and I am verily the Gracious, the All-Bountiful."

Should one, without mentioning the first part of this

verse, transcribe only the second, an uninformed person would fall prey to doubt and misgiving. Being regarded as a Branch, according to the explicit statement of the Blessed Beauty, is conditional upon turning towards and obeying the Centre of the Covenant and the Point of the Testament. Should, however, a Branch turn away, he shall grievously fall. As clearly stated with reference to Mírzá Muḥammad-'Alí, should he for a moment pass out from under the shadow of the Cause, he shall become a fallen creature. This explicit text, mentioning him by name and title, is from the Ancient Beauty, and Mírzá Muḥammad-'Alí himself doth accept and acknowledge its veracity. What deviation can be more severe than breaking the Covenant! Yea, to be regarded as a Branch is a divine bestowal, but one that is conditioned upon steadfastness in the Covenant. Violation of the Covenant would cause the Branch to fall.

3 For this reason, it hath been said in the fifteenth chapter of the Gospel of John: "I am the true vine, and my Father is the husbandman. Every branch in me that beareth not fruit he taketh away: and every branch that beareth fruit, he purgeth it, that it may bring forth more fruit." And further it is stated: "I am the vine, ye are the branches: He that abideth in me, and I in him, the same bringeth forth much fruit: for without me ye can do nothing. If a man abide not in me, he is cast forth as a branch, and is withered; and men gather them, and cast them into the fire, and they are burned."

Likewise, in the eighth chapter of the Gospel of John, 4 it is recorded: "They answered him, We be Abraham's seed, and were never in bondage to any man." It is then stated in the thirty-ninth verse of that same chapter: "They answered and said unto him, Abraham is our father. Jesus saith unto them, If ye were Abraham's children, ye would do the works of Abraham. But now ye seek to kill me."

In brief, according to the explicit Holy Writ, any soul, 5 even if of the highest rank and numbered among the Aghṣán, shall be brought to naught as soon as he violateth the Covenant. This is explicit in the text where, in clear reference to Mírzá Muḥammad-'Alí, even mentioning him by name and title, it is stated that should he for a moment pass out from under the shadow of the Cause, he shall be a fallen creature. And ponder how explicitly the same is stated in the Gospel.

This man hath not only broken the Covenant; he hath 6 also threatened the ruin of the Cause of God throughout all regions and brought humiliation upon the Faith of God. He was even intent upon shedding the blood of 'Abdu'l-Bahá, the documented proof of which is at hand. Furthermore, he falsified the Words of the Blessed Beauty. Obtain a copy of the declaration written by Áqá Mírzá Badí'u'lláh, and read it to see how he hath falsified the Book of God. The evidence of this, too, is at hand. As for thy second letter, thou shalt receive its reply in the world of dreams, and it is lengthy. Upon thee be greetings and praise.

60

He is God.

1 O thou servant of Bahá! What shall my pen recount? What shall I think? From the earliest days of the Cause, the Ancient Beauty, the Most Great Name—may my life be offered up for His loved ones—laid the foundation of the Covenant and the Testament upon a firm, fixed, and impregnable base, and made this lofty edifice of the Covenant the palace of the All-Merciful.

2 Whoso judgeth with but a little fairness will recognize that ever since the dawn of the world, until this heavenly Dispensation, no such Covenant and Testament hath ever before been established in the heights of the realms above or in the midmost heart of the Abhá Kingdom. From the earliest appearance of the resplendent Fire upon Sinai, until the setting of the luminous Day-Star of the Praised Beauty, no Sacred Text was revealed but that, whether explicitly or implicitly, it made mention of this Eternal Covenant and Ancient Testament, praised and commended those who hold fast unto it, and censured and admonished those who waver and violate it.

3 Then Bahá'u'lláh, with His own Pen, and tracing in His own hand glorious words across the snow-white pages, made a Covenant with all created things, visible and invisible, and called it "The Book of My Covenant", and set down in it these words: "The Will of the divine

Testator is this…"[100] One must be fair in judgement! Consider how carefully the Blessed Beauty proceeded. Even in the Kitáb-i-Aqdas, which hath abrogated all other sacred Books, He hath stated this theme in lucid and explicit language and not through allusion or symbolic terms, and hath expounded it, in numerous instances, with the utmost authority and power. Wherefore, shame be upon the foolish people because of whom we have been made the target of idle fancies and vain imaginings, nay, even been pierced by their spears and arrows of doubts.

But know this: The lamp of God shall be lit, and His 4 brilliant star shall shine upon the assemblage of humanity. His ocean shall surge, and the leviathan of the heavenly sea shall roar. The songbird of the rose-garden of Bahá shall warble with blissful rapture, and the nightingale of the bower of the Lord shall chant its eternal song. Thereupon shall the hearing ear, attuned to the song of the nightingale, hearken to the divine call, proclaiming: "Sanctified be the Lord! This is the songster of My paradise! This is the nightingale of My rose-garden! This is the candle of My worlds!" The glory of God rest upon thee.

61

He is God.

1 O thou who art steadfast in the Covenant! Thy letter was received and its contents noted. Speak in accordance with the instructions written herein, and utter not even one word more: Abraham, on Him be peace, made a covenant concerning Moses and gave the glad-tidings of His coming. Moses made a covenant concerning the promised Christ, and announced the good news of His advent to the world. Christ made a covenant concerning the Paraclete and gave the tidings of His coming. The Prophet Muḥammad made a covenant concerning the Báb, and the Báb was the One promised by Muḥammad, for Muḥammad gave the tidings of His coming. The Báb made a covenant concerning the Blessed Beauty, Bahá'u'lláh, and gave the glad-tidings of His coming for the Blessed Beauty was the One promised by the Báb. Bahá'u'lláh made a covenant concerning a Promised One Who will become manifest after one thousand or thousands of years. That Manifestation is Bahá'u'lláh's Promised One, and will appear after a thousand or thousands of years. He, moreover, with His Supreme Pen, entered into a great Covenant and Testament with all the Bahá'ís whereby they were all commanded to follow the Centre of the Covenant after His ascension, and depart not, even to a hair's breadth, from obeying Him.

2 In the Most Holy Book, there are two instances in

which He hath explicitly issued a binding command and appointed, in clear and unequivocal language, the Interpreter of His Word. In all His heavenly Tablets—especially in the Tablet of the Branch, the entire substance of which referreth to the servitude of 'Abdu'l-Bahá, that is, the Servant of Bahá—the Supreme Pen hath revealed all that is needed. And since 'Abdu'l-Bahá is the Interpreter of His Word, he sayeth that this Tablet of the Branch, that is, 'Abdu'l-Bahá, referreth to the servitude of 'Abdu'l-Bahá, and naught else.

In brief, among the characteristics of this Dispensation 3 which were not present in previous Dispensations, one is this: Bahá'u'lláh hath left no room for discord. For in His own blessed Day and by His Supreme Pen, He established a Covenant and Testament, appointed the Centre towards whom all must turn, explicitly specified the Interpreter of His Word, and closed the doors to false interpretations.

It behoveth everyone to render thanks unto God for 4 having granted such assurance in this blessed Dispensation, and for having left no cause for wavering. Therefore, all must show forth obedience and submissiveness towards that Centre and turn their entire attention unto him. As to thy speech, it must be confined to this and in no wise exceed it, so that it may foster harmony and ward off discord. The Glory of Glories rest upon thee.

62

He is the All-Glorious.

1 O thou who art enraptured by the sweet savours of God! Make haste, make haste towards the forgiveness and mercy of thy Lord! Press on, press on unto the wellspring of grace and compassion! Rush forth, rush forth to the fountainhead of bounty and favour! That is, arise to exalt the Word of God, to diffuse the sweet savours of God, to strive to spread the light of God, to kindle the fire of the love of God, to hold fast unto the Covenant and Testament of God, and to stand firm, by His gracious aid, in the Cause of God. It behoveth one such as thee to be even as a banner raised above all other banners, which waveth in the breezes of holiness wafting from the meads of the loving-kindness of thine Ancient Lord, and is set astir by the sweet-smelling fragrances that are shed abroad from the Abhá Kingdom. Glorified be my Lord, the Most High!

2 Thy letter, which testified to the firmness and constancy of the friends of God in the Covenant and the Testament, was perused and read out.

3 It is clear and evident that in every cycle and dispensation an implicit statement was made in order to safeguard the Word of Oneness, to preserve the Cause of God from harm, and to ensure the unity of all that are gathered beneath the shadow of the Divine Tree,

so that the impregnable stronghold of His Faith might remain safe and secure under the shadow of a single Word. While statements such as "Whosoever hath Me as his Master…"[101] were indeed allusions and not explicit, in this Most Great Dispensation a Divine Covenant hath been established, and the Book of the Covenant hath been revealed by the Most Exalted Pen. Mention hath been made of this ancient Covenant and mighty Testament in all the sacred Tablets and Scriptures, so that the Word of Oneness might be revealed and made manifest in all degrees and stations in the form of singleness, the light of Divine Unity might illumine the East and the West of the world of being, and all the peoples of the earth might gather round the same wellspring and be unified upon the same Path.

And since thou art well informed of the mysteries [4] enshrined in the Cause of God, thou must be vigilant at all times, lest the tempests of trials overtake feeble souls from any side, or the debilitating influence of vain interpretations and doubts cause the believers to waver. The glory of God rest upon thee.

63

He is God.

1 O my God! Verily, Thou hast created the universe and fashioned the human soul. Thou hast brought forth the entire creation and hast raised up all beings by the influence of Thine all-penetrating might. The Sun of the world of existence rose, with manifest splendour, above the horizon of the All-Praised. Ages passed and cycles rolled away, until the heaven of knowledge was again raised up and the earth of certitude was outstretched unto all, the ocean of bounty surged and the Luminary of the world shone resplendent, the stars of the world of creation gleamed brightly, the breeze of the All-Merciful wafted, and the full and brimming clouds of Thy grace and generosity rained down.

2 Holy realities—recipients of grace and light from the Day-Star of Truth—were raised up. They cast away their tattered garments, and through Thy bounty, O my All-Glorious Lord, they donned the robe of renewal instead. For Thou didst single them out to shed the splendours of Thy light, to set forth Thy commandments, to unveil Thy mysteries, to spread abroad Thy signs, to exalt Thy Word, to partake of Thine ocean, and to draw light from the fire of Thy oneness. These holy realities became the treasuries of Thy knowledge, the manifestations of Thy grace, the repositories of Thy mystery, the daysprings of

Thine inspiration, and the sources of Thy bounteousness. Thereupon did the tyranny of every envious one, the wrath of every contumacious one, and the bitter spite of every ungrateful one wax ever more severe against them. They all rose against Thy loved ones, whose only crime was detachment from all else except Thee, whose only misdeed was submission unto Thy Cause, and whose only fault was steadfastness in Thy Covenant. And this, verily, is what doth gladden the hearts of the faithful and devour the souls of the wicked. Verily, that which is light for the sincere ones is a raging fire for the adversaries of God.

Thou hast, O my Lord, fashioned immutable realities 3 in the world of existence and created beings of diverse natures. Thou hast desired naught for that noble species— the reality of the human soul—save that it should attain unto the most exalted station, perceive the signs, discover the testimonies, hoist the ensigns of Thy remembrance before all creation, lift up its voice and proclaim Thy name in the world of being, and diffuse the sweet savours of Thy holiness in this nether world—all this, so that its innermost being might mirror forth and reflect the image of the Concourse on high. Yet alas, souls remained heedless, and deprived themselves of the greatest bounty which Thou didst ordain in Thy realm. They bartered away the Joseph of Thy remembrance for the most paltry of prices, and stained his garment with the blood of vain imaginings. They repudiated Thy Covenant, cavilled at Thy Beauty, violated Thine honour, debased Thy Word, denied Thy wisdom, and hurled their calumnies upon Thy Countenance, all the while thinking themselves to be of them that are guided aright.

4   I implore Thee, O Lord my God, by Thy mercy, which is the source of all created things and the fountainhead of the entire universe, to lift the veils and bestow Thine abundant favours. Root out every trace of disloyalty, graciously aid all to be faithful, and grant that they may taste the sweetness of love and devotion, so that none may remain save those who bow down in adoration before Thee, and that darkness may vanish and pass away in every land. Thou art, verily, the Helper, the Almighty, the All-Glorious, the All-Bountiful.

5   O loved ones of God! The lamp of the Covenant is the light of the world, and its reality the gift of splendour; the star of the Testament is a shining moon, and the words traced by the Pen of the Most High a limitless ocean. The Lord, the All-Glorified, hath, beneath the shade of the Tree of Anísá (Tree of Life), made a new Covenant and established a great Testament. He hath summoned everyone to the loving embrace of His Beauty and announced unto all the revelation of His manifest verses. He hath subverted the foundations of discord and raised the edifice of divine favour. He hath kindled the light of guidance and, through the grace of the Abhá Kingdom, turned the world into a garden of delights. He hath made manifest the Eternal Covenant and hath appeared, cup in hand, at

the banquet of Revelation. He hath raised a mighty call and enabled every mindful soul to hear the celestial strains of the Covenant, so that the malicious might not breach the impregnable stronghold of the Cause or the ignorant taint its soft-flowing waters with the mire of idle fancies. He hath raised His summons in the midmost heart of the world and lifted the shrill voice of the Most Sublime Pen. In the East and the West, all ears have hearkened to the sweet accents of the Holy Spirit and discovered the purport of the Covenant and Testament.

Notwithstanding such clear, comprehensive, and explicit statements, certain individuals have begun to utter their own interpretations and have misconstrued the meanings after their own selfish passions and desires. They have defiled those perspicuous truths with vain and feeble imaginings and made His explicit command subject to unseemly conditions. What ignorance is this and what folly! What waywardness and what foolishness! They shut their eyes to the manifest Light and cling to the creeping things of the earth. They seek not the morn of guidance but abide in the darkness of faithlessness. They read not the clear and conclusive verses but spread feeble and vain interpretations. "Leave them to entertain themselves with their cavillings."[102] And abandon them to wander distraught in their drunken stupor.[103] They tell lies and falsehoods, tread the path of error, and see not that they are indeed drowning in the ocean of vain imaginings. And they shall soon know what lot awaiteth them!

7   O ye loved ones of God! Consider: Hath such a Covenant been established in any previous Dispensation, age, period, or century? Hath such a Testament, set down by the Pen of the Most High, ever been witnessed? No, by God! How will these people answer the Almighty Lord in the unseen realm? How would they reply if the Abhá Beloved should say: "O deprived ones! Did ye not hear the Call of the Testament? Did ye not see the clear words of the Book of the Covenant? Did ye not understand its explicit text? How then could ye deviate and cavil? Was the designated Interpreter not explicitly appointed in the Book? Was the Centre of the Covenant not plainly visible? Even if ye could not keep faith, why such treachery? Even if ye could not acknowledge him, why such haughtiness? Even if ye could not bear him allegiance, why such injury? Ye stabbed him with swords and daggers and aided every wicked doer. Ye hurled darts and arrows, and aimed spears and lances at him. No harm remained that ye did not inflict upon him, no slander that ye did not direct towards him, and no false tale that ye did not make the pivot of your complaints. Ye claimed light to be darkness and regarded guidance as error. Ye made a plaything of the Ancient Covenant, and considered the clear text of the Testament to be delirious ravings. The robe of the Joseph of the all-glorious and unseen Kingdom is dyed with blood, the raiment of the Ancient Beauty stained crimson."

8   O beloved of the Lord! Plaintive cries are raised in the Concourse on high, and ceaseless moans and lamentations

are the companions of the denizens of the Abhá Kingdom. All the peoples of the world are launching their assaults; all its nations and kindreds are hostile and contending. And in the midst of this field of tribulations standeth 'Abdu'l-Bahá, the target of every dart of tyranny. What is become of fairness and justice? Whither is gone the sense of decency and shame? Instead of being a healing salve for the wounds inflicted by the darts of the enemies, ye have aimed your knives at my throat. Instead of shielding me from the shafts of tyranny hurled by the nations of the world, ye have at every moment stabbed me and dealt a heavy blow upon my feeble body. Wretched is that which your hands have wrought! Woe betide you for having forsaken unity, chosen discord, broken the Covenant, and caused adversities to wax ever more severe. Verily will ye be driven to your Lord![104]

Briefly then, O ye that stand fast in the Covenant! [9] Render praise and thanksgiving to the Lord that ye abide beneath the canopy of the Covenant and are sheltered within the stronghold of the care and protection of the Day-Star of the world. The day is approaching when ye shall witness the violators of the Covenant retreating to the holes of disbelief and doubt, and creeping, worm-like, for shelter in the uttermost depths of the earth. On that day will the faithful rejoice.

Furthermore, as His Majesty the righteous King is [10] just and generous, and a helper of all kindreds and tribes, and as the Prime Minister promoteth the progress of the nation and is a sincere and trustworthy well-wisher of the throne, it is therefore our bounden duty to arise, with sincerity and goodwill, to fulfil that which is required, to show gratitude for such a gift. Perchance that noble country may be illumined, and that land may become the focal centre of the bestowals of the merciful Lord.

64

He is God.

1 O friend! It is a long time since any news hath been received from thee. Although, earlier, a letter arrived in which thou hadst asked a question, 'Abdu'l-Bahá hath been so deeply immersed in a sea of correspondence from every side that even if five scribes were at hand, the work could not be managed. All communication hath been severed for the past four or five years, and there hath thus been a slight wavering among some of the friends, some lapse in the diffusion of the divine fragrances, and certain idle thoughts in the minds of some. Therefore, continual communication must now be maintained with every region for some time, to make amends for the past interruption. And since thy question required a lengthy answer, the reply hath been delayed. Rest thou assured that, as soon as there is an opportunity, it will be written at once. Yet since I am drowned in an ocean of letters these days, and it is

imperative that I reply to the essential ones first, thou must wait until an opportunity doth arise. Thou art very dear to me, and I wish to respond to thy request....

Thou must be exceedingly alert, and shield the souls ₂ from veiled suggestions and secret whisperings. Enable them to be steadfast in the Covenant according to the explicit divine Text, which is a conclusive evidence of the Truth, so that Bahá'í unity may be preserved. Otherwise, a new sect would emerge each day, utter division would result, and the Cause of God would be destroyed—nay, exterminated. Were there any other power that could safeguard Bahá'í unity, I would have summoned every-one unto it. But ponder and reflect: Is it possible for the unity of the Faith to be protected by any other power than that of the Covenant? This is why I admonish every-one to cleave unto the Covenant—purely to safeguard Bahá'í unity.

Were one to consider the events of the previous cycles, ₃ the attempts to break the Covenant in this Dispensation are of no importance whatsoever. Sometime after Christ, Arius, the Patriarch of Alexandria, founded a new sect. He was an orator, articulate of speech and a very audacious and powerful person who succeeded in bringing one and a half million people under his influence. He even secured the allegiance of the Emperor Constantine. But since he deviated from the Covenant of Christ, at the end he faded away and perished. This Covenant was based on the words addressed to Peter, "Thou art Peter, and upon this rock

I will build my church."[105] And though these words attributed to Christ are based only on the report of some of His disciples, nevertheless Christian unity was preserved for eight hundred years through this implicit Covenant.

4   Now there existeth an explicit Covenant. It is not a mere verbal report. It hath been revealed by the Supreme Pen, Who openly addresseth the Covenant-breakers at its outset. He hath called it "The Book of the Covenant", a title written by His own Pen at the head of the Tablet. Then of what significance are the behaviour and conduct, the insinuations and whisperings, the interpretation and corruption of the Text by those who sow the seeds of doubt? At most it is this: They have only deprived themselves, and will continue to do so, and will fall into the darksome pit of "losing both this world and the world to come".[106] Every billowing ocean must needs produce foam, and all gold that is purified in fire leaveth behind some dross. Hast thou ever seen a surging ocean without froth, or pure gold that leaveth no dross behind in the consuming flame of fire?

5   The Qur'án hath explicitly stated this. He saith, and verily He speaketh the truth: "We have sent down the rain from Heaven; then flow the torrents in their due measure, and the flood beareth along a swelling foam ... And from the metals (that is to say, pure gold) that is molten in the fire, a like froth ariseth.... As to the foam, it is quickly gone: and as to what is useful to man, it remaineth on the earth."[107] Consider how explicitly this hath been stated.

The ocean of the Covenant shall eternally endure, and this is that which profiteth mankind. With but a single wave of it, this foam shall pass away like dross, leaving no trace behind. "Leave them to entertain themselves with their cavillings."[108]

The Lord be praised that thou art my cherished beloved, 6 my uniquely true and loyal friend. Thou must shield the Covenant and protect the souls lest they slip or waver. The Glory of Glories rest upon thee....

Examine carefully the commentary on the verse "In 7 the Name of God, the Compassionate, the Merciful".[109] Some of the meanings that thou seekest are implicitly contained therein, and it was praised by the Supreme Pen during His blessed days. Let then the masters of knowledge produce its like!

65

He is God.

O ye beloved of God! How great is this Dispensation! 1 How bright the effulgence of this Age, the Age of the All-Glorious Lord! All creation hath been set in motion, and the universe vibrateth with tidings of joy and ecstasy. The realities of all things are filled with blissful rapture, and every atom in existence is ecstatic with delight. Souls are attaining unto prosperity and advancement, and the friends are achieving success and progress. The light of Revelation is shining bright, and its signs are shedding light on all regions. The whole earth resoundeth with the praises of the greatness of the Ancient Beauty, and the Day-Star of His majesty shineth resplendent.

2   Every assemblage in the world is adorned with the mention of the Most Great Name, and every gathering of the kindreds and peoples of the earth is cognizant of the tidings of the advent of the Most Wondrous Luminary. The East is illumined by His light, and the West perfumed with His sweet savours. This dusty earth hath become a rose-garden through the outpourings of His bounteous favour, and the vast and lofty heavens are filled with delight through the splendours of His sun. The realities of all things have been quickened and revived, and the essences of all beings enraptured and enthralled. Goodly trees are growing and flourishing on every side, yielding sweet and luscious fruits. The banner of the Covenant is hoisted in every region, and the ocean of the Testament is surging with such endless billows and raging tempests as to cause every limb to quake.

3   In this Most Great Dispensation, the Ancient Beauty— may my soul be offered up for His loved ones—hath vouchsafed unto all the believers a sure testimony, a surpassing mercy and abundant favour, an infallible proof and clear evidence. In the Most Holy Book, which abrogateth all the Books and Scriptures of the past and standeth amongst them all transcendent and supreme, He hath, in

clear, explicit, and unequivocal terms, revealed the path and marked out the road to salvation. For five and twenty years did He nurture everyone, and fed them from the breast of holiness. In all His Tablets, Books, Epistles, and Scriptures, He made mention of the Covenant and Testament, praising the steadfast and extolling those who cleave tenaciously unto it, while condemning and rebuking those who waver, and even forewarning them of divine punishment and the threat of everlasting chastisement.

And then the Tablet of the Year of Stress, which is the 4 year of Bahá'u'lláh's ascension, was revealed and distributed in all regions.[110] In it He clearly and unequivocally stated the severity of the tests and the profusion of the trials. Some time thereafter, the Book of the Covenant and Preserved Tablet of the Testament was revealed by the Supreme Pen, wherein all were bidden, by His clear and explicit behest, to turn unto it and to observe, obey, and follow it, so that when the ocean of the tests and trials of the Year of Stress came to surge, no soul would be perplexed, dismayed, or confused; so that the straight path, the undeviating way, and the manifest light would become evident and clearly known; so that no room would be left for evil whisperings, no differences would arise, and the unity of the Word of God would be safeguarded.

Now a few capricious souls have appeared and begun 5 to engage in secret whisperings, and as soon as they feel sure of their target, they even openly voice their intentions. One of them saith: "The Blessed Beauty hath made us independent of aught else, and hath left no need unmet." The secret intent of such a statement is that there is no need for an appointed Centre. Another exclaimeth: "Infallibility belonged to the Blessed Beauty alone; no other person is infallible." His inner motive is to assert that the "the one whom God hath purposed" is liable to error. Furthermore, they say that one who was regarded with favour, who was a believer or the recipient of a Tablet during the days of the Blessed Beauty, cannot possibly be cast out. Their true objective is to hint that were such a person to arise in opposition, or be so bold as to show enmity, no harm would result. They spread talk of this sort both openly and privily. The whole purpose of these words is to violate the Covenant and Testament. This is that same clamour which the Beloved of the worlds hath foretold in all His Tablets.

6   O loved ones of God! Be wakeful, be ever wakeful! Be mindful, be ever mindful! For tests and trials are most severe, and the waverers are exceedingly subtle and destructive in their schemes. Outwardly they proclaim that they are the first to adhere to the Covenant, while secretly they strike an axe at the very root of the Tree of the Covenant and Testament.

66

He is the All-Glorious.

O thou dove of the rose-garden of faithfulness! O nightingale of the groves of praise to the Abhá Beauty! May the glory of God, His mercy, His bounty, and His praise rest upon thee.

That which thou hadst written with the pen of grief upon the page of woes was read and perused with the utmost attention. From its contents, brimming with bitter lamentation, the savour of profound sorrow and anguish was perceived. On the one hand, I was saddened; on the other, surprised and amazed. My sorrow was due to the intensity of thy sighs, whilst my surprise stemmed from the fact that this servant hath already written a number of letters to thee, dear friend, in all of which I expressed the utmost measure of love and affection. They were written in such wise that I imagined that such bliss and ecstasy would fill thy soul upon their perusal as to cause thee to rend asunder the raiment of the material world.

How is it that through a single word thou hast become so dispirited and dejected, so heartbroken and despondent? And yet, in this day, neither is praise the measure of honour, nor censure the sign of abasement and disgrace. Acceptance or denial, approval or rejection, all depend upon him whom God hath raised to serve His Cause and to exalt His Word amidst humankind. Know thou that all matters pertaining to the Cause revert to this servant. To none is given the right to reject or accept before hearing what this humble servant hath pronounced.

4   Forget then all these matters and, with the utmost resolve, firmness, and steadfastness in the Covenant of God, and with faithful adherence unto His Testament, strive to exalt His Word. Neither give ear to commendation and praise, nor be saddened or heartbroken by censure and humiliation. Arise amidst the peoples of the world and, wholly detached and sanctified from all save God and stirred by His Covenant and Testament, strive to awaken the heedless; for, in this day, most people are unaware and oblivious of the power of God's Covenant and Testament.

5   Although no explicit Covenant was established in any previous age or Dispensation, yet the followers of the Qur'án say that the Apostle of God—may the life of the worlds be offered up for His sake—stated at <u>Gh</u>adír-i-<u>Kh</u>umm: "Whoever hath Me as his Master, hath 'Alí as his Master."[111] Likewise, the Christians say that the One Who is the Spirit—may the soul of all existence be sacrificed for Him—addressed Simon, known as Peter, with these words: "Thou art Peter, and upon this rock I will build My church."[112] Now, in this Most Great Dispensation, the Covenant hath been conclusively established in clear terms and unmistakable language, leaving room for no interpretation whatever, in the Most Holy Book—a Book that abrogateth all the Sacred Scriptures of the past,

and whose laws have annulled whatever laws in other Tablets that are not in conformity with it. Furthermore, in the book of the divine Covenant and Testament, revealed by the Pen of Glory and named "The Book of the Covenant", Bahá'u'lláh entered into a Covenant with all created things. In all His Tablets and prayers, He hath made firm adherence to the divine Covenant and Testament to be the surest means of receiving heavenly bestowals, that all may apprehend the majesty and grandeur of that Covenant and Testament.

Now, some are conscious of the power of this Cov- 6 enant, and are firm and steadfast in the straight path, whilst others are not yet as aware of its significance as they should be. The sincere friends of the Blessed Beauty must strive to awaken the people. As this mighty, this impregnable stronghold shall remain inviolate and safe, let not thy heart grieve. All other matters are secondary and can be easily resolved with a word or two. Rest thou assured and hopeful, and remain firm and steadfast. The glory of God rest upon thee, and upon the beloved of the Lord.

Thou hast asked for permission to write of certain 7 matters. "Let thy sorrowful heart recount all that it desireth",[113] for my ears are attuned to thee.

67

He is God.

1 O thou seeker after Truth! Thy letter was received and thy purpose became known. Thou hast asked: If this divine Revelation is that same heavenly Kingdom which Christ said was nigh, then by what proof and testimony can this be demonstrated, and by what tidings can it be announced? There is no time for a detailed reply, so a brief account is provided.

2 Know thou that the proofs of the truth of this new Kingdom are the same as those of the Kingdom of Christ. The proof of the subsequent Kingdom is the same as that of the previous one—nay, it is the mightiest proof!

3 Proofs are of two kinds: those for the common people and those for the learned. The latter will not be convinced by the proofs for the former, who, likewise, will not be assured by the proofs for the latter. The common people seek miracles and marvels, while the learned regard these not as proof; these neither satisfy their search nor quench their thirst. Rather, they seek conclusive rational proofs. Thus, as thou art endowed with a keen vision and a sound mind, we will set forth conclusive and rational proofs that leave none the possibility for denial.

4 We say that the purpose underlying the advent of the Kingdom is the edification of the souls of men, the progress of the world of humanity, the manifestation of the

love of God, the establishment of fellowship and unity amongst all peoples, the appearance of divine perfections, and the realization of the glory of the human race. This is the purpose of the advent of the Kingdom, and this is its result. Observe, then, how the edifying power of Bahá'u'lláh hath enlightened the darksome East, transformed voracious beasts into heavenly angels, endowed the ignorant with knowledge, and caused ravening wolves to become as gazelles in the meads of oneness. Those who, because of custom or belief, rose in enmity against all peoples now associate with all in a spirit of perfect unity. Those who used to burn the Holy Bible out of exceeding ignorance now set forth the truths and mysteries of the Old and New Testaments. In a brief span of time, He so educated His followers that, even in chains and stocks, and under the threat of swords and blades, they would raise the cry of "Yá Bahá'u'l-Abhá!" and would offer sugar candy to their executioners that they might strike the final blow with sweetened mouths. Thou dost surely recall the story of Peter the disciple, and the crowing of the cock![114]

Another proof is that all the Persian divines and 5 prominent leaders in Ṭihrán know, beyond any doubt, that Bahá'u'lláh never attended any school, nor received any formal education, and from early childhood conducted Himself differently. Nevertheless, the divines and the learned of the East have testified to His extraordinary knowledge, wisdom, understanding, and perfections.

Despite their denial and bitter enmity, they still acknowledge that Bahá'u'lláh was a unique and peerless Figure of the age, although they do not recognize His sublime station as do the chosen ones and the sincere.

6   A further proof lieth in the very teachings of Bahá'u'lláh, which banish every trace of dissension and discord from the world of humanity, and establish everlasting unity and harmony. Refer to the Tablets of Tajallíyyát (Effulgences), 'Ishráqát (Splendours), Kalimát (Words of Paradise), Bishárát (Glad-Tidings) and Tarázát (Ornaments), and thou wilt clearly see what teachings have been vouchsafed by this new Kingdom—teachings that bestow upon the feeble body of the world a swift remedy and a practicable, lasting cure. The like of such teachings hath never before been witnessed.

7   Yet another proof is that it was from within this afflictive prison that Bahá'u'lláh revealed and advanced such a sublime Revelation—a Revelation whose renown hath spread throughout the world, which hath been firmly established in the East, and the light of whose radiant morn is diffused even as the rays of the sun. And all this despite the fact that the governments and peoples of the East arose in resistance and opposition, launching their attacks with every power at their disposal. Reflect: Hath such might and power ever been manifested before? What greater proof is there than this, that from within the prison walls He directed His mighty proclamations to the kings and rulers of the earth and foreshadowed, in unmistakable

terms, what the future would hold. He warned the great Emperor, then at the height of his power, of a sudden revolution, and predicted the downfall of his throne and the defeat and extinction of his empire.[115] And all this did indeed come to pass, as did the events foretold in Tablets and addresses directed to other rulers of the earth from within the prison confines. Behold with what power and majesty He manifested Himself from within a prison for robbers and murderers! What proof is there greater than this? To conclude, the proofs and evidences are many, but I have no time to write further.

And now, concerning the proofs sought by the unin- 8 formed masses: these consist of miracles and marvels. To state the matter briefly, there are many accounts of such marvellous feats associated with Bahá'u'lláh that are current amongst the people and could fill numerous volumes, were one to compile them. But since these do not constitute a conclusive proof for the contending denier, we will not relate miracles associated with Bahá'u'lláh. For the contenders may also relate such accounts from the idols of their fancy and base them on their own books and chronicles. We therefore present rational proofs, so that there shall remain no room for denial for any soul. The Glory of Glories rest upon thee.

68

1   O thou who art steadfast in the Covenant! That which was written by thy musk-laden pen brought great joy to our hearts. It imparted the glad-tidings of the cheer and exultation of the believers and the joyful news of the spirit of fellowship among the friends. God be praised that each one hath become even as a fruitful tree in the divine orchard, and doth stand as a swaying cypress upon the riverbanks of love and knowledge.

2   None had imagined that, despite the intensity of tests, those souls would remain happy and beaming with joy! This can be attributed to naught but the great bounty of God in these days—that in the depths of sacrifice, His loved ones stand firm and immovable and are constant and steadfast in the Covenant and Testament.

3   O God, my God! Assist Thou Thy servants who have found "at the fire a guide",[116] and have caught the light of the immortal flame kindled in the Tree of Sinai. Make them, O Lord, the signs of Thy Divine Unity amidst all people, and the emblems of Thy Oneness in Thy most exalted Realm. Give them to quaff from the wellspring of Thy mercy and from the clear waters flowing from Thy blissful paradise, that they may become inebriated with the wine of Thy love in the verdant meadows and vast gardens of Thy holiness. Assist them, O Lord, with the cohorts of the Supreme Horizon and the hosts of the Concourse on high. Thou, verily, art the Generous, the Compassionate,

the Lord of grace and bounty unto Thy feeble servants!
Thou, verily, art the Clement, the Merciful....

Thou hast sought permission for a visit. In these days, 4
the Holy Land is in turmoil by reason of the calumnies
spread by the slandering liars. For certain strangers from
amongst the non-believers have published some books,
filled them with countless calumnies, and distributed them
in these regions. 'Abdu'l-Bahá is therefore in dire peril
due to attacks from within and from without. Such are
the enemies of the Faith on the outside, and such the
violators of the Covenant on the inside. It is thus evident what commotion hath arisen. Yet, praise be to God,
through the unfailing grace of the Blessed Beauty, I have
remained firm in my position, have bared my breast to
the darts of malice hurled by every oppressor, and am
awaiting the onslaught of tribulations from every side,
that, wholly detached, I may hasten to the shelter of His
transcendent mercy.

Thou hast asked about the blessed Quranic verse "We 5
have given thee the twice-repeated seven."[117] The Muslim divines have interpreted the term "twice-repeated
seven" to refer either to the seven chapters of the Qur'án
that begin with the disconnected letters Ḥá' and Mím
or to the opening chapter of the Qur'án. They say it is
"twice repeated" because the opening chapter, consist-
ing of seven verses, was revealed twice—once in Mecca
and again in Medina—and, as such, it is twice repeated.
Furthermore, they say that as this opening chapter is

recited twice in the daily prayer, it is thus described as the "twice-repeated seven".

6   But the true meaning is the mystery of Divine Unity and the outpourings of heavenly grace, and that is the glad-tidings of the advent of the subsequent Revelation, in which the Bearer of the seven letters hath appeared twice. The first seven letters correspond to "'Alí-Muḥammad", and the second seven to "Ḥusayn-Alí".[118] This is the meaning of the "twice-repeated seven". Yet another meaning is that Muḥammad, the universal Manifestation of the Quranic Dispensation, together with thirteen distinguished souls, make fourteen, which is seven twice repeated.[119] There is no time for further elaboration. This is a brief but beneficial explanation.

69

He is God.

1   O Lord! O Thou Who graciously aidest whomsoever Thou willest, with whatsoever Thou willest, unto whatsoever Thou willest. Verily, that treasury of resignation, that wellspring of fidelity and fountainhead of purity—the honoured Riḍá[120]—fell prey to the cruel tyranny of the people of hatred and malice. He was, O Lord, sore-tried by the gravest hardships and the fiercest oppression of the perverse. He was held fast, time and again, in

the claws of ravening wolves and ferocious lions, until he fell into the clutches of a savage hound who tormented him with countless afflictions and weighed him down with galling chains. All the while, he raised his voice amongst the people, openly proclaiming Thy Name. Undaunted and undismayed, he never wavered in teaching Thy Cause. He feared not the scourge of the oppressors, nor was he frightened by the tribulations meted out by the vicious, the ignoble, the wicked, and the vengeful. He spoke with the utmost eloquence and presented the most wondrous proofs with manifest authority.

The hearts of those present were astonished by this 2 dignified man. They exclaimed, "He is indeed sincere and trustworthy, and speaketh the truth. He testifieth with absolute honesty and harboureth no secrets, for his account is but manifest truth without the least trace of dissimulation, false interpretation, or unsound commentary; it is indeed clear discourse concerning this great Cause."

The oppressors were assured that there was no mis- 3 chief, no wrongdoing or rebellion, and no secrets hidden and veiled from others, and yet they kept him confined to prison. Upon his release, he travelled to Qum, wherein rule the divines, they that are in grievous loss. There, once again, he was thrown into a fortified prison, in whose depths he languished for a long time, until at last God delivered him through the just intervention of a noble-minded man.

He never faltered or slackened in chanting the verses 4

of Him Who is Thy Remembrance and the Source of wisdom. Nay, rather, he hastened to the gathering of the evil-minded divines and set forth clear and manifest proofs. Hence the clamour of the clergy rose high, and they assailed him with grievous injustice. They cast him again into prison, subjected him to chains and fetters, and afflicted him with fresh torment. His weak and feeble frame, unable to sustain such dire hardships, yielded its life in this Path, and he reached Thy presence detached from all else but Thee, a guest at Thy Holy Threshold.

5   O Lord! Glorify the abode of This newly arrived guest. Grant him an exalted station within the precincts of Thy transcendent mercy in the presence of the glorious Companion; confer upon him a dwelling in that immeasurable and boundless immensity, the vast kingdom of Thy pardon and forgiveness, which none can comprehend save those whom the Omnipotent Lord hath inspired.

6   Verily, Thou dost bounteously favour whomsoever Thou willest, dost forgive whomsoever Thou willest, and dost pardon whomsoever Thou willest. There is no God but Thee, the Subtile, the Tender, the Ever-Forgiving, the Most Compassionate.

7   O honourable Majdhúb! That leader of the righteous is most dear to 'Abdu'l-Bahá. Whenever I find a moment, my thoughts turn again towards thee and I engage in prayer and remembrance on thy behalf. Supplications were likewise offered at the Divine Threshold, that God may bestow His unfailing grace upon His loved ones.

The Blessed Beauty is established upon the Throne 8
of Lordship, and we are all novices in the ranks of servitude and are linked together in thraldom to His Holy
Threshold. Nothing greater can be imagined for the
friends than to join 'Abdu'l-Bahá in servitude to the
Sacred Threshold. Since in His commentary on the Súrih
of Joseph, the Báb—may my life be offered up for His
sake—hath identified Joseph as the Manifest Beauty, the
true Joseph, and hath referred to Him as "our great and
omnipotent Master", then whenever thou readest it, thou
wilt but weep and grieve for the wrongs suffered by the
Blessed Beauty. This commentary is not currently at hand
for me to send to thee.

70

He is the All-Glorious.

O thou servant of the Ancient Beauty! When Joseph— 1
peace be upon him—unveiled his bright countenance in the Egypt of beauty, he set ablaze the souls of a
myriad buyers. Now the Joseph of the celestial Canaan,
the ruler of the Egypt of the spirit, with a face radiant as
the sun and a beauty far above the praise and description
of such as are endued with understanding, hath rent asunder the veils and emerged resplendent in the midmost
heart of the world. But alas, all the buyers have busied

themselves with the world of water and clay, have pursued their selfish desires, and have hence been deprived of beholding His Countenance and attaining His presence. Render thou thanks unto God that thou hast been among the buyers who seek that Divine Beauty, and among those who are enamoured by the Mystic Beloved. The glory of God rest upon thee and upon all those who have been enraptured by His Beauty.

71

He is God.

I O thou binder of books! Shouldst thou refer to the heavenly Books and Sacred Scriptures, and ponder the meanings enshrined therein, thou wouldst see that all their tidings and signs herald the advent of the Light of Truth and the Centre of Divinity. Forget not the tradition that saith: "Whatsoever is in the Torah, the Gospel, and other Scriptures is in the Qur'án, and whatsoever is in the Qur'án is in its Exordium, and whatsoever is in its Exordium is in the Basmalah, and whatsoever is in the Basmalah is in the Bá'."[121] But alas, for the eyes of the people are blind, and their ears are deaf. How well hath it been said:

To speak of the subtleties of Saná'í before the
    foolish and the weak of mind
Is like plucking the lute for the deaf or holding a
    mirror to the blind.

Gracious God! How strange, how very strange! The 2
people of the Book have withdrawn behind the veils,
whilst the common people comprehend the mysteries of
the Word. This is but a token of the bounteous favour of
my Lord, the Almighty, the All-Bountiful. Upon thee be
greetings and praise.

72

He is God.

Thou art He, O my God, Whose most beauteous 1
names and most sublime likenesses are sanctified
above the comprehension of such as pride themselves on
their knowledge of the realities of things, inasmuch as the
spiders of idle fancy can never weave the frail webs of
their understanding upon the loftiest summits to which
even the birds of human thought are powerless to ascend.
How, then, can such as are endued with insight discern
the mysteries of Thy Reality that is concealed from the
world of being? O Lord! Indeed, the inmost reality of all

created things can never hope to fathom the secrets even of the world of existence. How, then, O my God, can it apprehend the hidden Secret, the well-guarded Mystery, which is inscrutable to even the most luminous of realities in the realm of being within the invisible world?

2   O God, my God! The wings of human thought can never hope to ascend unto the Kingdom of Mysteries, and the minds of the righteous are sore perplexed in attempting to attain unto the gems that lie wrapt within the veils of concealment.

3   O Lord! The innermost reality of understanding in this contingent realm is, in its essence, utterly powerless to grasp even a single one of the mysteries of the All-Merciful, inasmuch as all understanding encompasseth that reality in the realm of existence that is comprehensible. How, then, could that which is contingent comprehend the Ancient Mystery unless the Ancient be encompassed by the contingent world? And how could this be possible, given that the encompassing one is greater than that which is encompassed, and the knower thoroughly comprehendeth that which is the object of knowledge? This being the case, how then can there be a path to Thee; how can there be a way to the Kingdom of Thy sanctity? Naught are we but mere helplessness and poverty in the face of the mysteries of creation, let alone before the sublime Reality, which is inaccessible to the realm of idle fancies and thoughts!

4   Thou hast, nevertheless, through Thine inestimable

grace and Thy resplendent bounty, and by virtue of Thy mercy that hath surpassed the whole of creation, fashioned a luminous Reality, a heavenly Being, a divine Essence—Whom Thou hast ordained to be a mirror, stainless and gleaming, that speaketh of the unseen world, that deriveth grace from that realm, and that shineth resplendently and copiously with the outpourings of those favours upon the entire creation. And this Thou hast done so as to deliver Thy sincere servants from the worship of idle fancies engraved even on the hearts of the mystic knowers. For verily, all Thy servants, O my Lord, except such as Thou hast chosen as Thine own, whilst communing with Thee, or bowing down in worship before Thee, conceive a fictitious reality comprehensible to their thoughts and minds. And thus do they worship it whilst immersed in the seas of idle fancies and vain imaginings. For, verily, Thine invisible and inaccessible Self can never be known; Thine unalloyed Essence can never be described. "The way is barred, and all seeking rejected."[122]

To whatever heights the most brilliant mind may soar, it can grasp no more than a mere token of the mystery of creation, a token which Thou hast deposited within the reality of all things. This, indeed, is the highest summit of comprehension to which those who inhabit the visible realm may hope to ascend, and even the manifold aspects of that token far transcend all comprehension in the realm of ascent.

6   All praise be to Thee, therefore, for having guided us to the Focal Centre of glory, the Manifestation of beauty, the Source of all light, the Dawning-Place of signs, and the Repository of Thy Revelation amongst the righteous. All praise be to Thee for having delivered us from idle fancies and vain imaginings, and for having rescued us from the worship of idols conceived by human minds. Thanks be unto Thee for having unlocked the gates of understanding to them who are well assured, and for having sent down from the heaven of Thy gifts that pure water which causeth the vales of the heart to overflow with the outpourings of the grace of God and the torrents gushing forth from the Focal Centre of mysteries.

7   O God, my God! Thou hast verily revealed the path, established the proof, and guided all to Thy glorious kingdom. Thy signs and mysteries have verily been diffused far and wide, the realm of realities hath been made to tremble and the limbs to quake, the sun and stars have been darkened, and the planets have been dispersed and fallen from heaven. For Thy testimony hath been manifested, and the Sun of knowledge hath risen. Every obscure mystery in the realm of creation hath been laid bare, and now, in this Day of Revelation, Thy Beauty doth shed its radiance with all-subduing potency upon the whole earth, shining with its all-encompassing power over king and subject alike. Every hearing ear hath hearkened to Thy call, and all holy souls have been quickened by Thy sweet savours. The influence of Thy Word hath verily encompassed the

righteous and the pious, and all tongues have testified to the majesty of Thy Revelation in this luminous age.

And yet, O my Lord, the company of deniers are veiled 8 from this manifest Light, and they that are estranged from Thee have turned away from Thy radiant countenance. They, indeed, are those that have failed to believe in Thy most exalted Beauty, the Manifestation of Thine own Self, the Embodiment of Thine incalculable and imperishable grace. How numerous the verses that have been sent down, the words that have been perfected, and the Scriptures that have been recorded; and yet the heedless have remained unconvinced of this mighty sovereignty, and the foolish are not satisfied by this ancient power. These clear and manifest tokens profited them not, nor did any of these Scriptures and scrolls of all-encompassing words avail them.

Thus it followed that Thou didst manifest Thine all- 9 subduing power over all created things, whereupon the Dayspring of Thine effulgent light withstood the onslaught of all the peoples and nations of the earth from within this Great Prison, and raised high His Word from under the weight of chains and shackles in this inaccessible fortress. The signs of His dominion have been diffused throughout the world, and the fame of Thy Cause hath been noised abroad and reached the most far-flung regions of the earth. And this verily is a shining proof, a conclusive testimony to those endued with sight as well as insight.

O God, my God! I beseech Thee by Thy manifold 10

bounties, through which Thou hast chosen the sincere amongst Thy creatures and favoured them over all that dwell on earth and heaven, to lift the veils from the eyes of men, to confer Thy bounty upon the righteous, to lead the heedless to the wellspring of guidance, and to cause them to tread this straight Path. Thou art in truth the All-Bountiful, the Almighty, and Thou art verily the Merciful, the Compassionate.

11   O thou who art firm in the Covenant! In all the Sacred Scriptures and Tablets revealed by the Primal Point—may my life be offered up for His sake—the supreme proof is the revelation of divine verses. Throughout all chapters of the Bayán, the Báb hath heralded the advent of Him Whom God shall make manifest. He hath not laid down any conditions for the appearance of that Most Great Luminary, but hath concluded every matter by encouraging and urging all to recognize the Beauty of the All-Merciful. Peruse thou the Bayán: Every one of its chapters endeth by cautioning souls not to remain veiled in the Day of His Revelation or, God forbid, to denounce and reject Him on the basis of the Bayán itself. For example, He saith, "Beware, beware, lest the Váḥid of the Bayán or that which hath been sent down in that Book shut thee out as by a veil from Him, inasmuch as it is but a creature in His sight." By "the Váḥid of the Bayán" is meant His blessed Being together with the eighteen Letters of the Living.[123] As to "that which hath been sent down in the Bayán", consider in what explicit and emphatic terms

He hath warned against being veiled by the Váḥid of the Bayán or by what hath been revealed in that Book.

It is obvious that the Primal Point—may my life be 12 offered up for His blessed Dust—was well aware of the Day of the Revelation and the identity of the Promised Beauty, that hidden Mystery and well-guarded Secret. This explicit warning was for the sake of emphasis, lest any soul should protest that the rejection of this Most Great Revelation by a certain person is reason for doubt and misgivings.

And yet, behold to what vain imaginings the people of 13 the Bayán are clinging.[124] They cry out: "Where is the primary school of Him Whom God shall make manifest?[125] Where are the kings of the Bayán? Where are its places of worship and its Witnesses?" However, by the same token, the followers of the Qur'án could also cry out and exclaim: "Where is the Great Catastrophe? Where is the Most Great Resurrection? Where are the darkening of the sun, the cleaving of the moon, the scattering of the stars, the heaving of the earth, and the rending of the heavens? Where are the levelling of the mountains, the gathering together of the beasts, and the boiling of the seas? Where are the Resurrection and the Judgement, the Bridge and the Balance? Where are the chastising angels, and where is the day that is reckoned as fifty thousand years in the sight of God? Where are Heaven and Hell? Where are the kindled fire, the paradise brought nigh, the river of life, the heavenly streams, the fountain of mercy, and the crystal waters? Where are the chastising angels and the guards of Hell? And where, and where, and where?"

14   The Exalted One—may my life be offered up for Him—hath said that on the day of His Revelation all these events came to pass swifter than the twinkling of an eye, and that "fifty thousand years" were traversed in a single hour.[126] If all these momentous events took place in a single moment, would not the school of Him Whom God shall make manifest reach its culmination within fifty years? Behold to what extent they remain captive to idle fancies!

15   The statement "or that which hath been revealed in the Bayán" is indeed meant to caution the people of the Bayán not to say, "Where are the kings of the Bayán, and where is the school of Him Whom God shall make manifest?" Great God! These people condition that Most Great Revelation upon His being admitted, like a child, into a primary school and regard this as the proof of the validity of His Cause. "But what aileth these people that they come not close to understanding what is said unto them?"[127]

16   Gracious God! After the martyrdom of the Báb—may my soul be offered up for the dust ennobled by His footsteps—in what way did that individual arise, and what actions did he undertake?[128] What eloquence did he evince and what wonders did he utter? All the loved ones of the Lord bear witness that, after the martyrdom of the Báb, this person vanished and went into hiding. He fled to the region of Núr, whence he scurried away—in the

coarse guise of a dervish—to the regions of Mázindarán and Gílán until he finally reached Kirmánsháh.

When the Blessed Beauty was being exiled from Iran, 17 despite the power of the king and the hatred and animosity of all its inhabitants, He arrived in Kirmánsháh in the utmost dignity. That individual did not have the courage to meet Him at that time. And when the Blessed Beauty reached Iraq, that person entered Baghdad secretly and in disguise, and took up residence in the Arab quarter, never daring to meet anyone. His sole accomplishment, his greatest feat, was to seek out a number of girls from here and there and marry them....

From the earliest dawn of the Cause until the day of 18 His ascension, the Blessed Beauty, openly and visibly, without any veil or concealment, withstood all the peoples, nations, and rulers of the world and exalted the Word of God. The Tablets to the kings were revealed, and the mystery of adoration was made manifest. In clear and unmistakable language, subject to no interpretation whatsoever, He directed His stern and explicit summons to most of the sovereigns. All the things that flowed from His Most Exalted Pen were fulfilled, one after the other. All that He foretold came to pass, His predictions were confirmed, and His warnings were proven true.

"Shall the darkness and the light be held equal?"[129] Nay, 19 by thy Lord, the Ever-forgiving! But the people "entertain themselves with their vain cavillings".[130] They see not, they hear not, neither do they understand.[131] "They call upon that beside God which can neither hurt them nor profit them. This same is the far-gone error! He calleth on him who would sooner hurt than profit him. Surely, bad the lord, and, surely, bad the vassal!"[132] The Glory of Glories rest upon thee.

73

He is God.

1 O servant of the one true God! In cycles gone by, although the signs of God's power and the truth of His Cause were clear and manifest, yet to outward seeming the divine tests were severe, and the ignorant found grounds for hesitation; for the Sun of Truth shone from behind subtle clouds, inasmuch as the advent of the Promised One was, according to the explicit and decisive terms of the Holy Text, subject to certain conditions. And as the common people, interpreting those Texts according to their literal meanings, found them contrary to their own understanding, they remained veiled and deprived.

2 For example, the advent of the Promised Qá'im was conditioned upon the appearance of the Dajjál,[133] of Sufyání,[134] of the invincible standard and the unsheathed sword, and of manifest sovereignty; upon the preceding of the Seven Goats and the flight of the dignitaries and

leaders of religion from all corners of the world to the Kaaba;[135] upon the appearance of astonishing signs, the victory over the East and the West, the submission of all peoples, the slaughter of the divines, and the turning of the seven mills by the flowing blood of those ignorant ones.

In the Gospel, too, the conditions for the advent of ₃ the Promised One are explicitly stated. They include the darkening of the sun, the eclipse of the moon, the falling of the stars, the quaking of the earth, the heaving of the mountains, the wailing and lamentation of the tribes of the earth, the coming down of the Promised One upon thick clouds, the descent of the hosts of angels, the blast of the trumpet, the call of the bugle, and the like. Thus, to outward seeming, they who failed to recognize Him had an excuse.

Likewise, the advent of the Great Resurrection was ₄ conditioned upon the quaking of the earth, the rising from the grave, the coming forth of the dead out of their sepulchres, the darkening of the sun, the cleaving of the moon, the scattering of the stars, the reduction of the mountains to dust, the assembling of the beasts, the rending of the heavens, the stretching forth of the Straight Path, the setting up of the Balance, the ingathering of bodies, the blazing of the nethermost fire, the adornment of Paradise, and the appearance of the maids and youths of heaven, the choice fruits, and the Maids of Heaven "whom no man nor spirit hath touched before".[136]

5   By all this is meant that the Resurrection was conditioned upon the appearance of all these signs. The Báb—
may my life be offered up for Him—hath said that all
these momentous events, and the Great Resurrection
itself, came to pass in less than the twinkling of an eye
and took place in the span of a single breath. And yet
not one soul perceived them or grasped their significance. But, praise be to God, in this Most Great Revelation no conditions have been set, no prerequisites have
been laid down, no veils exist, nor is there any excuse to
remain deprived.

6   It should first be noted that the Báb Himself—may
my life be a sacrifice for Him—addressing the greatest
pillar of the Bayán, hath said: "Beware, beware, lest the
Váhid of the Bayán or that which hath been sent down in
the Bayán shut thee out as by a veil from Him."[137] In other
words, take heed during the advent of Him Whom God
shall make manifest lest thou become veiled from recognizing Him by the Váhid of the Bayán itself, "inasmuch
as this Váhid is but a creature in His sight". That is to say,
the Váhid of the Bayán hath been created by Him Whom
God shall make manifest, and this Váhid consisteth of the
eighteen Letters of the Living and the Báb Himself—may
my soul be offered up for Him—Who is the nineteenth.
He hath furthermore cautioned him to beware lest he be
veiled from Him by the very words revealed in the Bayán.
That is, he should take care not to say that such-and-such
a statement in the Bayán indicateth that He Whom God

shall make manifest would appear two thousand years hence. Could an absence of conditions and prerequisites be stated in more unmistakable terms than this? Thus it is evident that in this Most Great Dispensation there is no cause whatsoever for anyone to be veiled.

The Báb—may my life be offered up for Him—hath 7 confirmed that the events of the Great Resurrection, which were to take place on the day that is reckoned as "fifty thousand years", occurred in less than the twinkling of an eye. And yet the people of the Bayán still protest, saying, "Why did the school of Him Whom God shall make manifest not endure? Why did He not gather together with the children, or study the alphabet, or become trained in the abjad?"[138] Consider how heedless they are and how foolish, how dull-witted and veiled.

Consider, moreover, how God's limitless power hath 8 appeared and been made manifest in this divine Dispensation. In the past, those who were shut out as by a veil would impute folly and impotence to the divine Manifestations. One would say: "Ye follow none other but a man enchanted";[139] another would cry: "He deviseth a lie about God, or there is a jinn in him";[140] and yet others would speak the words "And when they see thee, they do but take thee as the subject of their railleries. 'What! Is this he whom God hath sent as an Apostle?'"[141]

During the days of Christ, the people would protest, 9 saying, "O Mary! Thy father was not a man of wickedness, nor unchaste thy mother."[142] Likewise, in the Mosaic

Dispensation, the Pharaoh would say, "He, in sooth, is your Master who hath taught you magic."[143] And the chiefs among the people would scorn and scoff at the Prophets, saying, "We see not any who have followed thee except our meanest ones of hasty judgement."[144]

10   In this divinely appointed Day, however, in this heavenly age and spiritual century, none hath breathed such words as these. All the peoples and kindreds of the earth—whether Turks or Tajiks, Europeans, Africans, or Americans—have testified to the majesty and glory of the Manifestation of God. At most, they have denied the truth of His Cause and His station as a Manifestation; that is all. Today, in all the newspapers and publications of the world, civilized peoples bear witness to the greatness of the Blessed Beauty. Behold, then, how the might and power of the Word of God hath penetrated the very arteries and nerves of the body of the world.

11   Even the people of the Bayán have gained some credence in the eyes of others, through the pervading influence of the Cause of Bahá'u'lláh, the spreading rays of the Abhá Kingdom, and the irresistible power of the Word of God. For the people regard us all as members of the same community. For instance, when Mullá Hádíy-i-Dawlat-Ábádí was in the presence of the Wolf of Najaf in Iṣfahán,[145] he ascended the pulpit, and in order to save his own abject soul—I implore pardon from God!—he wholly recanted his faith in the Báb and cursed and reviled Him. His life was thus spared, and when he came to Ṭihrán he

became the embodiment of the words "They are deaf, they are dumb, they are blind and shall return no more."[146] Once the pervading power of the Cause of Bahá'u'lláh had penetrated the whole world, perfuming the East and illuminating the West; once the government had lost hope of exterminating it, and most people were secretly eager to become acquainted with the truth of the matter— then this individual and his kindred and relatives began to assert themselves before the notables and dignitaries in Ṭihrán and engaged in spreading their idle fancies. Since most people regarded us all as belonging to the same community, some from among the seekers accepted the claims of these individuals. The latter should have been grateful for this, but instead, they arose in denial and brought a myriad calumnies against the people of God, defaming them before friends and strangers. Soon shall they find themselves in manifest loss!

Moreover, it is known to friend and stranger alike, [12] and even to the people of the Bayán themselves, that after the martyrdom of the Báb, Mírzá Yaḥyá donned the headdress of a dervish and, with an alms-bowl in hand and a wayfarer's sheepskin cloak upon his shoulders, fled from Mázindarán, leaving all the friends in grave danger, while he himself roamed incognito and in the utmost secrecy in the regions of Mázindarán and Rasht. When Bahá'u'lláh finally reached Baghdad in the plenitude of majesty and glory, Mírzá Yaḥyá also arrived, but in secret and in disguise. And when the Blessed Beauty left for

Sulaymáníyyih, he worked and was known as a shoe merchant in Súqu'sh-Shuyúkh, Baghdad, Samávih, and Basra. Then, upon his return to Baghdad through Najaf, he assumed the name of Ḥájí-'Alíy-i-Láṣ-Furúsh, that is, the silk merchant.

13   No mention whatsoever of the Faith was heard any longer. But when the Blessed Beauty returned and proclaimed the Word of God, when His journey to Constantinople took place, the call and the fame of the True One were noised abroad, and there was no longer occasion for fear or peril—then everyone emerged from behind the veils, found a new arena, and flaunted himself. No one said: O valiant horseman of the arena of Cyprus, who hast sought British protection! Where hast thou been till now? Into what hole hadst thou crept during those eleven years in Baghdad? After the martyrdom of the Báb—may my soul be offered up for Him—what assistance didst thou render, what constancy didst thou manifest, and what steadfastness didst thou evince before the enemies? What action didst thou take, save to address so-called epistles to the Seven Witnesses, such as Mullá Ja'far in Káshán, Siyyid Muḥammad-i-Malíḥ in Ṭihrán, and others, at the end of each of which was written: "Send us a young maiden"? None of them, God be praised, ever sent any. In one letter was written: "God doth desire to behold thee amongst two thousand heavenly maidens", and so the number of his wives grew as much as possible. There was Umm-i-Aḥmad from

Shíráz, Badrí from Tafrísh, Ruqíyyih from Mázindarán, and several more from Baghdad. And yet, not content with these, he also wed the honoured wife of the Báb, the sister of Mullá Rajab-ʿAlí, known as the Mother of the Faithful, marriage to whom, according to the explicit statement of the Báb, was forbidden. A few days later, he passed her on to Ḥájí Siyyid Muḥammad.

No more mention was heard—no call, no remem- [14] brance or praise. The Cause of the Most Exalted One, the Báb—may my soul be offered up for Him—was effaced and obliterated. Had it not been for the return of the Blessed Beauty—may my soul be offered up for His loved ones—from Kurdistan, I swear by God, besides Whom there is none other, that no trace or name would have remained of this Cause. Friend and stranger alike testify to this.

And now that individual is, God be praised, living in [15] Cyprus under British protection, in comfort and happiness, while his hapless disciples in Ṭihrán have been induced, through empty promises and vain methods of divination, to stir up mischief and sedition against the government. He hath promised them that this and that will happen, and that through those foolish disciples, sceptre and crown will be granted. Thus have they all been entangled in the mesh of their own devices. Those hapless ones have been condemned to endless misery and eternal loss, whilst he liveth his days in the utmost comfort and tranquillity, with no fear or trepidation, no dread of peril or danger.

16   In short, the point is that these disciples, who raised such a clamour in Ṭihrán and were so confident in his promises, should have asked him to deign to go to Ṭihrán himself, to act as a true leader and commander, and to issue such incitements and provocations from there. The Manifestations of God and His Chosen Ones have always been the first to carry out that which they enjoin upon others. Yet this individual, while dwelling in peace and safety in his retreat in Cyprus, hath sent his hapless disciples to the cannons and the gallows. Were anyone to gaze with the eye of fairness, this fact alone would suffice. The Glory of Glories rest upon thee.

74

He is the All-Glorious.

1   O ye who are staunch! O ye who stand firm! When the light of Divine Essence dawned above the horizon of Singleness, the splendour of His Oneness shone forth and the daysprings of existence were illumined with manifest grace. So radiant was the light of that Sun of Truth, and so abundant the outpourings of the clouds of His bounty, that the soil of all beings, even as a fertile field, became the bearer of the mysteries of all that hath been and shall be. Those mysteries lie latent and preserved in the innermost reality of the soil of existence and are

manifested according to the capacity of the world, bringing forth jasmine and lilies, verdant grass and sweet herbs.

Those whose icy breath and whispers are as cold as 2 midwinter have now spread in all directions, carrying leaflets of doubt, hoping to wither the soil of the hearts with the biting chill of Covenant-breaking, so that the seeds of divine wisdom that God hath deposited therein may decay and perish. But how far, how very far from the truth! For the glowing fire of the Covenant hath so set the world ablaze that no frost or ice can withstand it for a moment. This, verily, is the truth.

Wherefore, O friends of God, gird up the loins of 3 endeavour, and be so enkindled by the Lord's burning Fire as to light up the East and the West in such wise that every Covenant-breaker would be put to flight and every wavering soul would take heed. Such a great bounty dependeth on unity, harmony, and concord among the beloved of the Lord. The friends in that region must grow so intoxicated by the wine of unity that they become even as a single sea. Though its waves be many, the sea is one; diversity is not an obstacle to unity.

Praise be to God, for ye are all illumined by the same 4 Sun and are all brightened by the same Light. Ye are inebriated by the same cup and seek holy ecstasy in the same tavern. Ye are, one and all, enamoured by the countenance of the same Beloved and are captivated by the charm of the same Beauty. Ye quaff from the same wellspring and taste the sweetness of the same draught.

5   It behoveth every one of you, however, to show the utmost consideration unto the revered Hands who are foremost in service, for they are the dawning-places of the manifold bounties, loving-kindness, and favours of the Blessed Beauty.[147]

75

He is God.

1   O beloved servants and handmaidens of God! In its weakness and frailty, the world of humanity is even as a heap of darksome dust. Yet when the clouds of mercy of the All-Knowing Lord rain down upon it, this dark earth shall bring forth crimson flowers and shall become the resplendent rose-garden of the Concourse on high. Although we are weak and feeble, yet the bounties of the Blessed Beauty are boundless and inexhaustible. In offering gratitude, we have no recourse but to confess our own shortcomings, no remedy but to hold our peace, for we are powerless and wanting, feeble and faltering. Wherefore, praise be to the Lord of creation, through Whose bounty these helpless ants show forth the strength of Solomon, and these needy and feeble gnats become royal falcons of the heights of mystery, causing the bestowals of the Almighty to be manifested.

2   Now, concerning the recorded tradition that in former

times only two letters were revealed but in the days of the Qá'im all the remaining ones shall be made manifest, the following is meant. All the works and sciences, laws and ordinances, inventions and wonders, and the perfections of the human world that had been manifested in bygone times, were even as two letters. But in this wondrous Dispensation, and with the appearance of the glorious Treasure, the perfections and attainments of the world of humanity and its limitless sciences and arts shall advance to such a degree that they may be likened unto all the remaining letters.

That is, this wondrous Dispensation is so different 3 and distinguished from the previous ones that, even as ye witness, though it is still the first century, so many mysteries of creation have, within so short a period, stepped forth out of the realm of the invisible into the visible world. How many well-guarded secrets once enshrined within the realm of the unseen have been revealed! How many discoveries have been made of the hidden realities of things, and how many inventions and wonders have appeared! Infer then from this what the future shall hold.

Await the break of His sovereign morn,
These are but effects of its early dawn![148]

The Glory of Glories rest upon you.

76

He is the All-Glorious, the Most Effulgent.

1 O thou who art firm in the Covenant! The opening of thy letter bore the words: "O 'Abdu'l-Bahá!" What a call this was, for it caused my heart to leap with joy and my soul to tremble with delight. Glad-tidings encircled me on every side, my eyes were cheered, and my whole being breathed in the sweet savours of a garden of roses. This call, even as the melody of the Concourse on high, filled the soul of 'Abdu'l-Bahá with joy and rapture.

2 By Him Who hath illumined my face with the light of absolute servitude to His Holy Threshold! No melody can fill this yearning soul with such joy and rapture as the call of "O 'Abdu'l-Bahá!" And no sweet accents warbled by the birds of the orchards can thrill my heart with such delight as the dulcet tune of "O 'Abdu'l-Bahá!" This melody causeth my heart to leap with joy, and these wondrous words fill me with blissful rapture, but only on condition that this name be accompanied by no other epithets of praise, and paired with no other titles. The designation should be "'Abdu'l-Bahá" alone for it to bestow boundless joy upon my heart and soul. This is my qualification and my station, this is my title and my glory, and this indeed is my highest aspiration throughout eternity.

3 Thou hast commended the beloved of the Lord, saying that they are fully occupied with worship and praise,

are seizing the Cup of the Covenant, and, elated with joy at the banquet of the Lord, are unloosing their tongues in gratitude to the All-Merciful. This, indeed, is as it should be, for in this day there is no other path for the friends, and no other testimony for the pure in heart.

I beseech and entreat the all-pervasive grace of the 4 Most Bountiful Lord to grant that the hearts of His loved ones may become the repositories of divine inspiration and the dayprings of the effusions of His limitless bounty, so that, with the utmost harmony and fellowship, they may all be freed from the estrangement of the realm of vainglory and may associate with one another with perfect humility and lowliness. May no trace of self be detected from their conduct and manners, from their words and deeds. Man's greatness lieth in humility, and his abiding glory is found in lowliness, self-effacement, and servitude to the servants of the Lord. This, verily, is the greatest attainment in this resplendent Day.

Thou hast asked concerning the blessed verse "From 5 the heaven to the earth He ordereth all things, and hereafter shall they come up to Him on a day whose length shall be a thousand of such years as ye reckon."[149] By this "day" is meant the Day of the Great Resurrection, the Day of Judgement, for on that Day there shall appear such signs and events, such splendours and occurrences, marvels and wonders, truths and mysteries, precepts and writings, that the revelation of those splendours and signs cannot be contained even in fifty thousand years. Moreover, the precepts and laws, and the writings, teachings, and manifold bounties associated with that Day, which is none other than the "appointed time of a known day",[150] shall remain valid and binding for a full thousand years, nay for five hundred thousand years. Such a span of time is merely an approximation that alludeth to ages and centuries. And on that appointed Day, the outpourings of divine grace shall visibly descend from the kingdom of mercy and the heaven of oneness. And as such outpourings of grace cannot endure forever in this nether world, that glorious light must needs return to the luminous Star from whence it came, and those merciful showers that emanate from the liberal effusions of the sea of oneness must return, once again, to the Most Great Ocean.

6   Even as thou hast witnessed, in the day of the appearance of the Point of the Qur'án—may my soul be offered up for Him—the splendours of God's manifold grace shone forth, clear and manifest, through that luminous Day-Star upon the whole of creation, and for a thousand years that heavenly grace was vouchsafed unto all lands and regions and unto the realities of all created things. And when that Dispensation drew to a close, those signs and splendours returned to the unseen realm.

7   And then, a new Day dawned and a wondrous light shone forth. The Morn of Oneness rose, and the Day-Star of the world gleamed bright. The Most Great Ocean surged, and its billowing waves mounted to the Concourse on high. The clouds of bounty gathered above,

and the showers of mercy rained down. The light of truth appeared, and the way of guidance was made manifest. The glorious testimony was disclosed, and the path of the All-Merciful Lord became plain and evident. Through the limitless grace of the Divine Springtime, the Abhá Paradise was made to adorn the Most Exalted Kingdom. The bounties, the splendours, the mysteries, the signs, the verses, and the proofs of this wondrous Light that hath hoisted its banners on this joyous Day shall remain in effect for five hundred thousand years.

By thy dear life, I have no time to write more; other- 8 wise, I would have written a wondrous commentary, a mighty book, on this blessed verse. The glory of God rest upon thee.

Notes

1 Shoghi Effendi, *God Passes By* (Wilmette, IL: Bahá'í Publishing Trust, 1974, 2018 printing), p. 398.

2 Shoghi Effendi, p. 387.

3 Shoghi Effendi, pp. 387, 381.

4 A reference to Adrianople.

5 Mullá Ḥusayn-i-Bushrú'í.

6 The Arabic Bayán 1:7.

7 The Báb's Tablet to Mullá Báqir-i-Tabrízí.

8 "Mirror" was a title bestowed by the Báb on several of His followers.

9 See Kitáb-i-Aqdas, ¶175 and note 185.

10 Qur'án 4:78.

11 Qur'án 2:2.

12 Qur'án 33:40.

13 His turban.

14 Cf. Qur'án 20:108.

15 A reference to Mírzá Hádíy-i-Dawlat-Ábádí.

16 Qur'án 10:41.

17 Cf. poem by Abu'ṭ-Ṭayyib al-Mutanabbí.

18 Qur'án 76:21.

19 Mírzá Muḥammad-'Alí, 'Abdu'l-Bahá's half-brother.

20 Bahá'u'lláh.

21 The Báb.

22 A reference to the Afnán, the relatives of the Báb.

23 The cistern adjacent to the Shrine.

24 "Signs" and "Proofs" are references to the Muslim clerics.

25 Light.

26 Mírzá Yaḥyá; an allusion and contrast to "Yaḥyá the chaste", the Islamic title of John the Baptist (see Qur'án 3:39).

27 Qur'án 38:42.

28 *Murgh-Mahallih* means "Abode of the Birds".

29 A reference to *God's Heroes*, a play written by Laura Dreyfus Barney and published in 1910.

30 Mírzá Ja'far, the son of Maḥmúd-i-Sharí'atmadár-i-Láhíjí.

31 Cf. poem by Naẓírí Nishápúrí.

32 The *English Churchman*, a Protestant newspaper, had published articles opposing the Faith, including one by Rev. Peter Z. Easton on 20 September 1911.

33 Cf. Qaṣídiy-i-Varqá'íyyih, an ode revealed by Bahá'u'lláh in Kurdistan.

34 Cf. Rúmí.

35 A reference to Mírzá Ḥusayn Khán, the Iranian Minister in Constantinople.

36 Qur'án 9:33.

37 Cf. Psalms 132 and 48.

38 Cf. Qur'án 22:11.

39 A reference to Constantinople.

40 Cf. Qur'án 26:227.

41 An allusion to a verse by Rúmí.

42 The Azalís.

43 The attempt on the life of the Shah by Ṣádiq-i-Tabrízí.

44 A character, infamous for his moral laxity and indifference to honour and fidelity, mentioned in Ottoman Turkish sources.

45 A reference to Fáṭimih, the second wife of the Báb.

46 A reference to the prohibition in Qur'án 4:23 against marriage to two sisters at the same time.

47 Poem by Naẓírí Nishápúrí.

48 See note 26.

49 Cf. Qur'án 22:12–13.

50 Mírzá Yaḥyá was one of those on whom the Báb had bestowed the title of "Mirror".

51 Constantinople.

52 9 August 1919.

53 Adrianople.

54 Constantinople.

55 Qur'án 12:16.

56 Ḥáfiẓ.

57 Egypt.

58 An allusion to a poem in Arabic: "We can learn from those who went before us in bygone centuries."

59 Jesus.

60 Qur'án 14:24.

61 The original name of Peter.

62 Rúmí.

63 The ascension of Bahá'u'lláh.

64 An allusion to the story of Joseph in Qur'án 12:31.

65 Qur'án 7:128 and 11:49.

66 A reference to the 'ulamá and their fomenting of political upheaval in Iran.

67 A reference to the activities of the Azalís in Constantinople.

68 Jamálu'd-Dín-i-Afghání.

69 A reference to an allegation advanced by Mírzá Muḥammad-'Alí against 'Abdu'l-Bahá.

70 The Tablet, addressed to Siyyid Mihdíy-i-Dahají, is quoted in the Will and Testament of 'Abdu'l-Bahá. The full text of this statement is "Should he for a moment pass out from under the shadow of the Cause, he surely shall be brought to naught."

71 Qur'án 22:73.

72 Kitáb-i-Aqdas, ¶53.

73 A reference to Mírzá Yaḥyá's two sons-in-law Mírzá Áqá Khán-i-Kirmání and Shaykh Aḥmad-i-Rúḥí.

74 Kitáb-i-Aqdas, ¶53.

75 Jesus.

76 Cf. Qur'án 54:2.

77 Qur'án 17:82.

78 Qur'án 15:29.

79 Qur'án 68:4 and 9:3.

80 Imám Ḥusayn.

81 Caliphs of the Umayyad dynasty.

82 Ṭihrán and Khurásán.

83 Abraham.

84 Moses.

85 Jesus.

86 Muḥammad.

87 Qur'án 25:41.

88 An allusion to Rúmí's story about a jackal that fell into a barrel of paint and then claimed to be a peacock.

89 Qur'án 59:19.

90 Cf. Qur'án 21:74.

91 Qur'án 38:11.

92 Ancient communities mentioned in the Qur'án.

93 Qur'án 3:190.

94 Qur'án 2:18 and 8:31.

95 Qur'án 2:105 and 3:74.

96 Qur'án 33:21.

97 Matthew 16:18.

98 See note 70.

99 A reference to the second Bahá'í Teaching Convention of the Central States, held in 1919.

100 The full sentence reads: "The Will of the divine Testator is this: It is incumbent upon the Aghsán, the Afnán and My Kindred to turn, one and all, their faces towards the Most Mighty Branch."

101 A reference to the Ḥadíth that the Prophet Muḥammad delivered a sermon at Ghadír-i-Khumm in which He stated: "Whoever hath Me as his Master, hath 'Alí as his Master." The Shí'ihs consider this verbal statement to be authoritative and on its basis believe 'Alí to be the lawful successor to the Prophet.

102 Qur'án 6:91.

103 Cf. Qur'án 15:72.

104 Cf. Qur'án 75:29–30.

105 Matthew 16:18.

106 Qur'án 22:11.

107 Cf. Qur'án 13:17.

108 Qur'án 6:91.

109 'Abdu'l-Bahá's commentary on "Bismi'lláhi'r-Raḥmáni'r-Raḥím", the opening words of nearly all the chapters of the Qur'án.

110 The Lawḥ-i-Saniy-i-Shidád. The numerical value of Shidád ("Stress") is 309, which denotes the year of the passing of Bahá'u'lláh according to the Muslim lunar calendar (A.H. 1309/A.D. 1892).

111 See note 101.

112 Matthew 16:18.

113 Rúmí.

114 Matthew 26:34.

115 Napoleon III.

116 Qur'án 20:10.

117 Qur'án 15:87.

118 In Persian and Arabic, as vowels are not written, these names each consist of seven letters.

119 By "thirteen distinguished souls" is intended Muḥammad's daughter Fáṭimih and the twelve Imáms.

120 Probably Mullá Muḥammad-Riḍá of Muḥammad-Ábád.

121 A reference to the opening chapter of the Qur'án, which begins with the letter Bá'.

122 From a Ḥadíth.

123 A Váḥid has a numerical value of nineteen.

124 Bábís who rejected Bahá'u'lláh.

125 See Kitáb-i-Aqdas, ¶175 and note 185.

126 See Qur'án 70:4.

127 Qur'án 4:78.

128 Mírzá Yaḥyá.

129 Qur'án 13:16.

130 Qur'án 6:91.

131 Cf. Matthew 13:13.

132 Cf. Qur'án 22:12–13.

133 The Antichrist, who it was believed would appear at the advent of the Promised One, to contend with and be ultimately defeated by Him.

134 Another figure who it was believed would raise the banner of rebellion between Mecca and Damascus at the appearance of the Promised One.

135 According to Islamic tradition, Seven Goats would, on the Day of Judgement, walk in front of the promised Qá'im, and their deaths would precede the impending martyrdom of their true Shepherd.

136 Qur'án 55:56.

137 Addressed to Vaḥíd in the Tablet to Mullá Báqir-i-Tabrízí.

138 The ancient Arabic system of allocating a numerical value to letters of the alphabet, so that numbers may be represented by letters and vice versa.

139 Qur'án 17:47.
140 Qur'án 34:8.
141 Qur'án 25:41.
142 Qur'án 19:28.
143 Qur'án 20:71.
144 Qur'án 11:27.
145 Sh̲ay<u>kh</u> Muḥammad-Báqir, denounced by Bahá'u'lláh as the "Wolf".
146 Qur'án 2:18.
147 A reference to the Hands of the Cause appointed by Bahá'u'lláh.
148 Anvarí.
149 Qur'án 32:5.
150 Qur'án 56:50.

Index